Banks and industrial finance in Britain
1800–1939

New Studies in Economic and Social History

Edited for the Economic History Society by
Michael Sanderson
University of East Anglia, Norwich

This series, specially commissioned by the Economic History Society, provides a guide to the current interpretations of the key themes of economic and social history in which advances have recently been made or in which there has been significant debate.

In recent times economic and social history has been one of the most flourishing areas of historical study. This has mirrored the increasing relevance of the economic and social sciences both in a student's choice of career and in forming a society at large more aware of the importance of these issues in their everyday lives. Moreover specialist interests in business, agricultural and welfare history, for example, have themselves burgeoned and there has been an increased interest in the economic development of the wider world. Stimulating as these scholarly developments have been for the specialist, the rapid advance of the subject and the quantity of new publications make it difficult for the reader to gain an overview of particular topics, let alone the whole field.

New Studies in Economic and Social History is intended for students and their teachers. It is designed to introduce them to fresh topics and to enable them to keep abreast of recent writing and debates. All the books in the series are written by a recognised authority in the subject, and the arguments and issues are set out in a critical but unpartisan fashion. The aim of the series is to survey the current state of scholarship, rather than to provide a set of prepackaged conclusions.

The series has been edited since its inception in 1968 by Professors M. W. Flinn, T. C. Smout and L. A. Clarkson, and is currently edited by Dr Michael Sanderson. From 1968 it was published by Macmillan as *Studies in Economic History*, and after 1974 as *Studies in Economic and Social History*. From 1995 *New Studies in Economic and Social History* is being published on behalf of the Economic History Society by Cambridge University Press. This new series includes some of the titles previously published by Macmillan as well as new titles, and reflects the ongoing development throughout the world of this rich seam of history.

For a full list of titles in print, please see the end of the book.

Banks and industrial finance in Britain 1800–1939

Prepared for the Economic History Society by

Michael Collins
University of Leeds

CAMBRIDGE
UNIVERSITY PRESS

Published by the Press Syndicate of the University of Cambridge
The Pitt Building, Trumpington Street, Cambridge CB2 1RP
40 West 20th Street, New York, NY 10011-4211, USA
10 Stamford Road, Oakleigh, Melbourne 3166, Australia

Banks and Industrial Finance in Britain 1800–1939 first published by
The Macmillan Press Limited 1991
First Cambridge University Press edition 1995

Printed in Great Britain at the University Press, Cambridge

A catalogue record for this book is available from the British Library

Library of Congress cataloguing in publication data

Collins, Michael, 1946–
  Banks and industrial finance in Britain: 1800–1939 / prepared for the
Economic History Society by Michael Collins.
     p.   cm. – (New studies in economic and social history)
  Originally published: Houndmills, Basingstoke, Hampshire: Mac-
millan, 1991. (Studies in economic and social history).
  Includes bibliographical references and index.
  ISBN 0 521 55271 0 (hc). – ISBN 0 521 55782 8 (pb)
  1. Finance – Great Britain – History. 2. Banks and banking – Great
Britain – History. 3. Monetary policy – Great Britain – History. 4. Capital
market – Great Britain – History. I. Economic History Society. II. Title.
III. Series.
HG186.G7C574   1995   95–18745
332.1′0942–dc20   CIP

ISBN 0 521 55271 0 hardback
ISBN 0 521 55782 8 paperback

Contents

Acknowledgements

I am indebted to those who offered comments on, and made corrections to, the manuscript. Many thanks to Michael Edelstein, Ranald Michie, Forrest Capie, Katrina Honeyman, Sue Bowden and John Hillard. I am also grateful to Nick Crafts and Leslie Clarkson for their early encouragement.

1

The nature of the problem

Have the banks failed industry? In Britain there has long been a sizeable body of opinion that has believed so. Throughout this century economists and other commentators have expressed doubts about the role played by British monetary institutions in providing the financial services – especially the provision of long-term finance – essential for nourishing a modern, competitive industrial sector. For these critics, financial deficiencies are seen as a serious weakness in British economic development.

Doubts first arose towards the end of the nineteenth century and beginning of the twentieth century when the UK began to face increasingly stiff competition from other industrial nations and such doubts have resurfaced whenever British industry has been seen to be performing badly. At the time of World War I criticism was levelled at the failure to finance large-scale industrial combines of the sort that the enemy, Germany, was apparently so successful at promoting (Foxwell, 1917). During the interwar period, the banks were condemned for not doing enough to promote the extensive restructuring of industry which many thought essential if the country was to recover its export markets and reduce the abysmally high rates of unemployment (e.g. Clay, 1929, *186–9*). In the post-World War II period, too, the inadequacy of financial provision has often been highlighted as a serious contributor to Britain's relatively poor growth performance (e.g. Carrington and Edwards, 1979).

There is no doubt, then, as to the long-standing nature of the charge against the banks. At the same time, the banks have always had their own champions who have hotly denied allegations of failure. In a nutshell, the whole question remains controversial. It is important, therefore, to weigh up the arguments on all sides. Moreover, the longevity and importance of the debate means it is essential to do this within a proper historical as well as theoretical perspective. This will not only allow an assessment of what happened in the past but should also enhance understanding of the present performance of the British economy.

(i) The meaning of 'failure'

The debate on the role of financial institutions has to be seen in the much broader context of anxiety over Britain's growth record – over the loss of industrial hegemony at the turn of the last century and over the economy's chronically poor performance relative to that of other industrial nations throughout most of the twentieth century.

Much of the case rests on *a posteriori* reasoning (i.e. arguing from effect to cause). The 'effect' in this case is the UK's growth record which is widely accepted as having been 'unexceptional-to-poor'. It has been common to argue that for a mature economy such as the UK, the pace of growth is largely set by the performance of the industrial sector, especially manufacturing, where the potential for productivity gains is high. Yet, in aggregate, British performance has been poor. Two major deficiencies have been identified which have a direct bearing on the role of banks. The first is the comparatively low rate of investment in the UK; and the second is the allegedly lower take-up rate of new technology. Now, there are many possible explanations for these two features of British economic history – the poor quality of British entrepreneurs, the low level of technical education and training, factor availability and the inflexible attitude of the labour force are four of those commonly canvassed – but deficiencies in financial provision have been to the fore amongst potential 'causes'.

The banks' detractors believe that the type and adequacy of financial services supplied can seriously affect the rate of capital accumulation (and this, in turn, is generally associated with the rate of obsolescence). True, the greater provision of bank funds for industry will not in itself be sufficient to ensure a high rate of investment (industrialists might not take up funds even if they were available) but it is seen as an essential prerequisite (industry will not be able to invest more if the funds are not available). The strength of the argument rests heavily on international comparison, for it is alleged that in other capitalist countries financial institutions have more actively promoted the provision of long-term funds for industrial investment. Moreover, in some cases and in some periods, the banks in these other countries appear to have protected their commitments by taking a more active role than their British counterparts in the management and strategic planning of the businesses of industrial clientele. In these countries, it is claimed, there has been closer cooperation between the financial and industrial sectors (sometimes under the auspices of the state) and this has been successful in fostering economic growth. In Britain, on the other hand, it is widely accepted that throughout most of the past century-and-a-half the main financial institutions – the deposit banks, the discount houses and the merchant banks – have concentrated on short-term credit provision and/or on holding their longer term assets in the form of government and public utility securities (from both home and abroad). They seem to have shied away from long-term loans and investments to domestic industry and it is this which is said to have been to the detriment of industry. It is in this sense that banks are alleged to have 'failed' industry.

Underlying this claim is a view of how markets work, about the possibility of market failure over the very long term. The money and capital markets can be likened to other competitive markets in which demand and supply are reconciled and price and the allocation of resources determined. Seen from a neo-classical perspective it seems incredible that over a number of months, or years (let alone decades or centuries!) unsatisfied demand would not provoke a positive response on the supply side to the profitable opportunities so created – surely suppliers would act to increase their profits by correcting any obvious deficiency? In fact, if you believe that markets – including British financial markets – work quite well, then it is simply not credible that British industry could have been constantly demanding long-term capital (creating a potentially profitable opportunity for those banks prepared to meet the demand) which profit-making financial institutions refused to supply. In effect, acceptance of the rationale of markets – with the usual assumptions of rationality, optimality and of profit-maximising – denies the possibility of bank 'failure' in this area. In fact, in this particular case, it is often suggested that the absence of certain financial services probably reflected the lack of demand for them rather than any failure on the supply side. It is likely, so those who believe in the efficacy of markets argue, that the demand of British industrialists for funds from outside their companies was either insignificant or was being met from sources other than the banks. On this line of argument, then, if banks did not provide long-term industrial finance there were sound market reasons for not doing so – there was no large volume of unsatisfied demand. In general, therefore, an important group of economists, and the logic of a widely used body of economic theory, would deny that the banks could have failed industry.

In contrast, the banks' critics are much less sanguine about the effectiveness of competitive forces and, from a variety of standpoints (outlined in the next chapter), they allege that serious market failure has indeed occurred. All these allegations hinge, to some degree, on a belief that the potential for a higher rate of industrial investment has, indeed, existed in the UK over a very long period, but that banking practice frustrated its realisation. For the critics, either the market failed to provide the opportunities in which those seeking industrial funds could effectively signal their demand, or financial institutions proved insensitive to the market opportunities so created: i.e. that the market for financial services was neither perfect nor efficient.

To reiterate, differences in the approach to the effectiveness of market forces – whether a particular commentator is optimistic or sceptical – underlie much of the division of opinion that exists over the question of whether or not the banks failed British industry.

2

Explanatory schema

Before looking at the debate in any detail, it will be useful to categorise the various theoretical explanations that have been offered for the failure of British banks to develop sufficiently their provision of industrial capital. Below, three types of schema, or models, are distinguished although it will become obvious that there is a great deal of overlap between them.

(i) Early start thesis

The term 'Early Start Thesis' is usually applied to a line of argument dealing with Britain's economic performance in general. Within this general analysis it is claimed that the fact that the UK was the first country to industrialise created disadvantages in later years, compared with those countries which made a late start on the path to industrialisation. The allegation carries with it a strong implication of market failure in the sense already discussed – an allegation that once patterns of economic relationships, institutions and policy are well established they are resistant to change and, as a result, do not behave 'efficiently'. In the specific case of financial markets, it has indeed been common to claim that a fair degree of inflexibility developed. That once established, historical patterns of banking practice and policy persisted beyond the time when they were most appropriate to the economy's needs.

One of the most formal statements about the impact of 'early start' on the nature of financial provision was put forward by Alexander Gerschenkron in the 1960s (Gerschenkron, 1966). In fact, Gerschenkron's main concern was with those European countries which industrialised after the UK, but his analysis carried strong implications for the 'early starter' and it has coloured many of the later comments on British financial development.

Gerschenkron envisaged a staggered sequence of national industrial revolutions. Britain's was the first, with 'great spurts of industrialisation' following in other European nations after varying time intervals. For Gerschenkron, relative timing was critical. The longer it was before a particular country industrialised, the more economically backward it would be relative to existing industrialised nations. As a result, each new industrialiser faced circumstances differing, at least in degree, from those that had confronted its successors: on the whole, the degree of competition on world markets would be more intense; the scale of operations needed for establishing a successful industrial sector would be that much greater; over time, too, an increasing technical sophistication would be required, and so on. In other words, the longer it took before an industrial revolution was experienced, the more 'economically backward' the industrial newcomer would be on the eve of its own industrialisation.

According to Gerschenkron, this state of relative economic backwardness carried fundamental implications for the nature and course of the development process itself and accounted for some of the most important national differences in the way economic development has been carried through. Such national differences are far-reaching, embracing the particular forms of economic institutions and relations established within a country. Especially relevant was the prominence Gerschenkron accorded to national differences in financial institutions and markets.

Gerschenkron's view of the relationship between financial development and economic backwardness can be illustrated from the contrast he drew between Britain and Germany. Following the conventional wisdom of the time, Gerschenkron accepted that Britain had undergone an industrial revolution in the late eighteenth/early nineteenth centuries and that Germany had not experienced a 'great spurt' until the 1860s.[1] On the eve of her industrial revolution Britain had not been economically backward but, on the contrary, had been amongst the industrial leaders of the eighteenth century and had already experienced a long period of agricultural and commercial expansion. One consequence was that there existed substantial sources of funds independent of the banks and these could be utilised to finance development. Moreover, for the most part the fixed capital needs of the nascent industrialists of the late eighteenth and early nineteenth centuries were not onerous. The standard of technology was crude compared to what was to come later, in most cases the scale of production was small (in workshops rather than factories) and, as the new British products did not have to face competition from existing suppliers endowed with superior technology and market share, the whole process of technical change was relatively gradual and within the means of most British industrialists to finance. As a result the demands on British banks for long-term industrial capital were few. Instead the banks concentrated on augmenting the existing supply of media of exchange (e.g. by issuing notes), improving the means of remittance and meeting customers' short-term credit needs. The requirements of the economy thus gave rise to the creation of the British 'credit bank' system.

Gerschenkron contrasted the fact that German industrialisation occurred much later, at a time when British industrialists already enjoyed market dominance and technical superiority in many areas. German entrepreneurs thus had to establish industrial plants both large enough and sufficiently well equipped to be able to compete with the more advanced economy of Britain. Consequently, their fixed capital requirements were larger, so large that internal funding was not feasible. According to Gerschenkron, from an early stage German industrialists had to turn to financial institutions for funds. From the onset of the industrialisation process, then, strong financial–industrial links had to be forged. Moreover, German banks played a leading role (at least, initially) in the strategic planning of industrial development. For instance, they were active in promoting greater concentration of ownership and a larger scale of production within heavy industry, two developments Gerschenkron uncritically accepted as beneficial in the period up to World War I. In Britain there was no marked industrial reorganisation or concentration movement 'because of the different nature of relations between banks and industry' (Gerschenkron, 1966, *15*). By implication, then, the failure of British banks to do the same for British industry was detrimental.

To reiterate: according to this line of argument, Britain's 'early start' meant that the country developed a banking system that was appropriate to its needs at the time of the industrial revolution but one which was to become less suitable to the requirements of a maturing economy.

The weakness in this case, though, is the absence of a convincing explanation for the alleged immutability of early institutional arrangements and financial relations. Over the decades, why did they not alter in such a way as to meet more satisfactorily the perceived requirements of the economy? Why did British banks not meet industry's fixed capital needs if this is what was required? It is crucial to the case for those who allege market failure on this scale and over such a long period, to explain *why* financial institutions proved so unresponsive.

(ii) Institutionalists

In many respects Gerschenkron's comments on UK financial institutions are indirect (secondary to his concern with the more backward economies of the nineteenth century) but others have been much more explicit in both their allegations and their explanations. One such group of critics are those who can conveniently be grouped under the heading 'Institutionalists'. The general concern of this group has been with Britain's overall long-term economic performance but part of the analysis deals specifically with financial provision.

A recent statement of this view emphasises two aspects of British economic history (Elbaum and Lazonick, 1986, *1–17*):

(i) First, it is argued that the form of industrial development in the nineteenth century differed markedly from that of the twentieth century. During last century British markets tended to be atomised, with numerous suppliers operating on a relatively small scale and with easy access to these markets for newcomers. Individual firms were often small, usually owned and managed by the same people (frequently within the one family); and their products were often differentiated and produced in small batches to customised orders. The twentieth century, on the other hand, has belonged to corporate capitalism, with mass production techniques and scientific management, with an emphasis on standardisation, managerial controls and the ready acceptance of new technology.

(ii) The second feature that is emphasised is that whereas nineteenth-century Britain may have developed institutions appropriate to the type of industrial production of the day, those institutions proved unable to generate a successful transformation to forms more suitable to corporate capitalism. In this, Britain lagged seriously behind countries such as the USA, Germany and Japan.

In many regards, then, the 'institutionalist' case is a variant of the 'early start thesis' – the UK is seen to have suffered from decisions taken during her early experience of industrialisation. It is also open to much the same criticism – namely, given the obvious rewards for change and adaptation in the 'right' direction (higher rate of growth for the economy as a whole, higher profits/lower costs for individual market agents), why did it not happen? The strength of the argument, though, rests on the fact that the UK's long-term growth record has indeed been poor in international terms. Moreover, supporters of this view point to the individual case studies which seem to confirm that there were serious problems involved in the application and adaptation of many factors considered important for successful adoption of mass-production techniques.

Elbaum and Lazonick deny that these failings arise solely from the innate conservatism of the British people – after all, many other societies (Japan and South Korea, to take just two examples) have successfully broken through the barriers imposed by traditional society. Instead, they emphasise the reactionary, constraining influence of the institutions and institutional relations established during the nineteenth century. 'Britain's distinctiveness derived less from the conservatism of its cultural values *per se* than from a matrix of rigid institutional structures that reinforced these values and obstructed individualistic as well as collective efforts at economic renovation' (1986, 2). Nevertheless, the manner in which institutional rigidity *autonomously* inhibits industrial development is not clear from their analysis. In fact, despite claims to the contrary, it is very difficult to imagine general institutional structures having reactionary effects which were independent of society's cultural conservatism. The difficulty in drawing out the distinction is sharply increased by the meaning given to 'institutional structures'. The institutionalists interpret this very widely and, in practice, it has come to resemble the extensive list of economic, social and political 'failings' that has long been current amongst critics of British capitalist development. Thus, amongst other factors, Elbaum and Lazonick point to deficiencies in education and training, in industrial relations, in the attitudes of trade unions, in managerial techniques, in the structure of markets, in the role of the state and in the implementation of government policy.

Within this list, financial provision has also been singled out as culpable. Here, the main criticisms have been that:

(i) British financial institutions have concentrated on short-term credit creation, having persistently shied away from providing long-term funds for industry.

(ii) City of London institutions have exhibited a strong predilection for holding overseas assets and financing international trade. They have been much less involved with domestic industry.

(iii) City institutions have successfully influenced exchange rate and monetary policy to their own advantage. Thus, for long periods, the authorities have favoured high or stable exchange rates and 'dear money' and this has operated to the detriment of domestic industry.

(iii) Financial interests within a socio-political context

A number of studies have been inspired – either directly or by way of reaction – by Marxist models of capitalist development. Of direct relevance has been the concern with the extent of class cohesiveness amongst British capitalists. At the beginning of the century Rudolf Hilferding characterised the later stages of capitalism as experiencing a distinct concentration of economic and political power into the hands of industry, with a corresponding demise of commercial and landed interests (Hilferding, 1910).

He envisaged the closest cooperation between financial and industrial capitalists in this process, with the banks in a dominant position as the suppliers of funds and the effective arbiters on competing claims for finance. At this stage of capitalism, the interests of industrial companies and banks would converge, perhaps with common directorships and the closest possible co-operation to secure markets and boost profits.

The central proposition of the thesis, the drawing together of industrial and financial interests, has appeal. It seems a reasonable expectation that industrialists and bankers would find cooperation mutually advantageous as the scale and complexity of the industrial process gathered pace. It could be imagined that industrialists would have found internal funding increasingly inadequate, with capital from the financial institutions an obvious alternative. In turn, the banks could boost their own profits by meeting this demand. Moreover, on a more general level, the long-term prosperity of the financial sector (as for the whole economy) would seem more secure if growth in the industrial sector were buoyant, not constrained through lack of financial provision. As a theoretical proposition, therefore, the prediction that industrial and financial capital would come close together has much to commend it.

Yet Hilferding himself was fully aware that at the time he was writing there existed a clear divide between British banking and industrial interests. He argued that this was a result of Britain's early industrial dominance but he predicted that as international competition increased, UK industrialists would move towards larger scale production and the concentration of market power. In the process, banking and industrial interests would converge to form what he termed 'Finance Capital'.

Subsequently, a number of writers have adapted Hilferding's basic thesis to explore the apparent drawing together of banks and industry at different periods in British history (e.g. Rubinstein, 1977; Overbeek, 1980). However, most commentators have been intent on showing that concepts of capitalist class cohesion are not an accurate representation of the historical record in the UK. Instead, they claim that the capitalist class has been much more splintered and they argue that the financial interest has generally operated against that of industrialists. It is this, they posit, that accounts for the long-standing division between banks and industry.

A common starting point is to stress that Britain's position as an international financier has been at least as important in determining the course of her economic history (Ingham, 1984, *ch. 1*). Throughout the nineteenth and twentieth centuries the financial institutions of the City of London have been heavily involved in the intermediation of international trade and finance (e.g. in the provision of sterling bills before 1914, in their dominance of the commercial insurance market, in their commitment to the Sterling Area from the 1930s to the 1960s, and in their operations in the euro-currency markets of the 1970s and 1980s) and this, it is claimed, drove a wedge between the banks and domestic industry. For a start, it meant that the profits of British financial institutions were much less tied to the fortunes of domestic industry. More critically, though, it created a broad conflict of interests. City institutions fostered policies designed to promote international trade and finance and to enhance their own role within the multi-lateral payments system that emerged from the nineteenth century. In particular, they espoused free trade (opposing suggestions of tariffs and other restrictions on imports into the UK), the main-tenance of international currency convertibility, stable exchange rates and sound monetary policies at home. In contrast, critics claim, British industry's interests lay in the creation of some form of protection from overseas competition, in the maintenance of a more buoyant and prolonged expansion of domestic demand than was often possible within a fixed exchange rate regime and in securing (if not from the banks, then from the state) adequate funds to finance long-term investments.

Critics would allow that there were circumstances when the interests of the two groups of capitalists coincided (in their mutual desire to restrain wage costs, for instance) and that, on occasions, serious dislocations to the international economy (e.g. during the 1930s and immediately after World War II) forced the temporary abatement of City influence. Nevertheless, the assertion is that conflict between City and industrial interests is a fair representation of modern British economic history, and of the development of economic policy. Moreover, this is true even if many industrialists themselves have not always realised it, or have even denied it and given support to the objectives of the banking interest. Latter-day critics would argue that industrialists were mistaken in this – they were unable to see the broad and long-term perspective that is observable to the historian or retrospective sociologist. In other words, like the 'Institutionalists', this diverse group of writers takes a supra-market view that transcends the claim of the neo-classical analysts that competitive forces would have ensured financial provision appropriate to the economy's needs. For them, the broad social, economic and political interests of the financial sector offer a more accurate means of explaining the relationship between banks and industry than the rather facile analysis of competitive markets.

It is important to appreciate that these critics claim that the conflict between the City and industry has not been narrowly economic. In Britain's case, they say, the financial interest has secured the more dominant political, social and ideological influence. It has been the ideology of 'the City' which has more successfully secured positions within the elite of British society, including civil servants and politicians responsible for government. On questions of policy central to their own interests, British financiers are said to have generally found it possible throughout recent times to enlist the active support of the state, with industrial interests consigned a more subordinate position.

To reiterate, a large group of writers, who have adopted a broad sociological approach to the question of British financial provision, argue that the banking interest has been largely distinct from the industrial interest. Finance has not been dependent on domestic industry for its livelihood. Moreover, the City's influence over policy – over the dominant economic ideologies in the UK – has been damaging to long-term industrial growth. In this broad sense, the banks are said to have failed industry.

The rest of this book examines the history of financial provision in the UK, with most attention on the critical periods of the nineteenth century and the interwar years. In working through these chapters the reader's tasks of assessing and categorising various strands of evidence and opinion will be easier if they can be related to the theoretical explanations outlined above. Do competitive market forces offer sufficient explanation? If not, does the answer lie in Britain's legacy as an early industrialiser? Have the specific forms of institutions and institutional relationships adopted in the UK imposed major rigidities on the role of banks? Has the broad social, political and economic structure of the country driven a wedge between finance and industry and operated against the industrial interest? Or does the explanation lie in a combination of some or all of these schema?

3
Industrial finance before 1870

As Britain was the undoubted world industrial leader prior to the late nineteenth century it could be argued (although it does not necessarily follow) that the banks at that time were not seriously inhibiting industry's potential. Allegations of serious financial deficiencies from the last quarter of the nineteenth century, therefore, beg the question: what changed?[2] Was it the banks or industry? Was it that banks once met industry's needs (in the successful pre-1870 years) but that subsequently banking practice changed in such a way as to force an estrangement with industrialists? Or was it rather that industry's financial needs altered significantly and that the banks failed to react in an appropriate manner? In other words, did the banks of the late nineteenth century actively withdraw from a previously supportive role for industry or was their role a more passive one in which conservative banking practices did not respond to changing demand from industrialists?

The search for an answer to this question would seem to lie in straightforward historical investigation. Why not study the internal archives of the banks of the period (and those of their industrial customers) and so establish the historical record? The practical problems, however, are immense. For much of the nineteenth century there were hundreds of banks in the UK: in 1825, for instance, there were 715 banks; in 1850, 459; in 1875, 381; and even in 1913 there were still 88 (Collins, 1988a, 52). Moreover, for the great majority of them, the most useful of their records (account books, etc.) have, unfortunately, been lost to the historian. It is also true that the further back in time one goes, the greater the problem (Pressnell, 1956, 2–3); Collins, 1984, 43–5;

Goodhart, 1972, *13–70*). So a definitive historical picture cannot be directly compiled. Instead, historians have had to rely on patchy information about the form in which banks held their assets, about the type of loans and investments made. This surviving information falls into three main categories: business records of the banks, business records of their customers, and public pronouncements made by contemporary bankers and other informed commentators (e.g. before parliamentary enquiries or in financial journals). A fundamental problem with these sources is that their collection is not random. As a result it can be very difficult to know how 'typical' any one example or opinion may be, a problem made inherently worse by the local nature of banking throughout most of the nineteenth century. Thus, if information were available on the type of loans made by a bank based in an industrial town such as Dundee or Middlesbrough, it could be very rash to generalise to banks operating in predominantly commercial centres (e.g. Liverpool) or agricultural areas (Kings Lynn) or, indeed, the City of London.

Inevitably, then, creation of 'the historical record' has sometimes involved assumptions and assertions based on rather scant empirical evidence. As a result, the picture that has emerged of actual banking practice is far from complete or incontrovertible. For instance, the central issue of how much – and in what form – the 'typical' bank lent to industry is not known with any degree of precision. Instead, historians have had to rely upon piecemeal quantitative data, bolstered by evidence of a more impressionistic and indicative sort. This is true even for the years immediately prior to World War I, but it has posed more serious difficulties for students of the previous century and a half when the traditional form of British banking was being developed.

(i) Early industrialisation, 1760–1830

It has been widely accepted that during the 'industrial revolution' period (1760–1830 approximately), the relatively small scale of industrial operations and the basic standard of technology employed meant that for most industries the need for short-term funds to finance working capital outweighed that required for fixed capital (plant and machinery, etc.) (Pollard, 1964; Crouzet, 1972, *36–9*; Chapman, 1970). As Sidney Pollard emphasised in a pioneering article: 'Thus [for the early industrialist] the problem of finding capital was largely a problem of finding circulating capital for stocks of raw materials, work in progress, and finished commodities, and for rents, interest and wage payments, and the like . . .' (Pollard, 1964, *305*). Industrialists at that time were inclined to use the firm's own internal funds (undistributed profits) and/or money from friends and acquaintances to finance fixed capital requirements, rather than borrow from financial institutions. As a result the demand on banks for long-term industrial funds were not great (Cameron *et al.*, 1967, *35–59*; Crouzet, 1965; Gerschenkron, 1962, *11–16*). Instead the main requirement was for short-term credit in the form of short-period loans, overdrafts (or cash credits in Scotland) and bill discounts.

From the supply side, too, there may have been persuasive arguments in favour of concentrating on short-period credits. For the most part, banks at that time were small businesses whose fortunes were closely tied to those of the local community. In fact, in England and Wales the Bank of England's monopoly of joint-stock banking was not curtailed until 1826 and this prevented banks from having more than six partners (in Ireland, a similar privilege for the Bank of Ireland was not removed until 1821). Even in Scotland, where larger partnerships were permitted, banks were fairly small and locally or regionally based. This was also to be the case for the early joint-stock banks in England. In addition, the banks' main liabilities (notes and deposits) were held by the general public and were potentially subject to immediate, or short notice, withdrawal. At the time, in fact, sudden large-scale withdrawal was no mere theoretical possibility – bank runs or panics were part of most bankers' experience. In the crisis of 1825–6, for instance, 93 banks in England and Wales (or some 15 per cent of the total) found themselves unable to meet the demands of their depositors and note-holders for cash and had to suspend payments. Even by the middle of the nineteenth century severe short-term shocks were a real possibility. By this time bank failures were less common but liquidity crises – even as late as 1866 and 1878 – were still capable of administering major jolts to the commercial banking sector.

Deposit banks of the late eighteenth and early nineteenth centuries were thus small and vulnerable. It was essential, therefore, for them to maintain an asset structure of sufficient liquidity. In effect, they were obliged, first, to maintain at least a small-holding of cash in their tills (so as to meet customers' everyday needs for currency). Secondly (and of more significance to the present study) as a safeguard against extraordinary demands for cash from depositors and note-holders, they would have had to ensure that sufficient of their loans and investments were capable of being quickly recalled and/or encashable through resale (often to other bankers). It was within this category of liquid assets that bills of exchange (and later, Consols) came to epitomise the 'ideal' British bank asset. On the other hand, long-term loans or investments to industrialists (or anyone else for that matter) were not liquid because they could be neither readily resold without loss nor quickly recalled.

On *a priori* grounds, therefore, the heavy reliance of British banks on potentially volatile deposit (and note) liabilities would suggest that the provision of long-term loans could not be allowed to dominate bank portfolios. They had to avoid 'tying up' too large a proportion of their assets in case they should need to liquidate them quickly in order to pay off liabilities. But this did not preclude a well-managed bank from maintaining a 'judicious' percentage of assets in liquid form while, at the same time, committing a 'safe' portion to longer term investments. The incentive for holding some assets in this illiquid form, of course, was profit – normally, a higher rate of interest could be charged on longer term loans.

What was considered 'judicious' or 'safe' would have been a matter of judgement and would have varied from bank to bank and over time, but it seems a safe assessment that the generality of banks would have provided some long-term finance. Now, given that the demands from industry for such funds are said to have been rather restricted, the proportion of bank assets so committed may well have been adequate to industry's needs in this early period of industrialisation. This, indeed, is the consensus view. Despite the pressures on banks to maintain a liquid portfolio, in general there does not appear to have been a serious supply constraint for industrial loans during the industrial revolution.

In fact, there are numerous individual examples of bank loans being made to industrialists throughout the period (Pressnell, 1956; Mathias, 1973). Typically these loans were for small amounts but on occasions they could be for substantial sums. Sometimes they were fixed period loans, often they were rolled-over credits. A recent study of the important West Riding wool textile industry concludes that such bank loans played a critical role in sustaining the industry over the period 1750–1850 (Hudson, 1981, 1986). However, the piecemeal nature of the evidence continues to make it very difficult to quantify the significance of bank loans to industry in general. It has been suggested, though, that their importance transcended the mere question of quantification. According to Peter Mathias it was having access to bank credit at particular times that could prove crucial to the early industrialist: 'when a business was being established for the first time; when cash and longer term credits were needed to enable it to survive a depression; when a major step forward was required in expansion which was beyond the scope of current profits or accumulated reserves' (Mathias, 1973, *135*).

In sum, then, most historians agree that during the late eighteenth and early nineteenth centuries, British banks were indeed 'credit banks' but that the role of these banks in industrial development was nonetheless important. Industrialists' requirements for outside funds were mainly for short-term credits and the banks met these via loans on current account or through bill discounting. Moreover, access to such bank credit may have been critical to some industrial and commercial firms at times of pressure. The final and important point is that, although banks were generally governed by concerns over liquidity, there are many individual examples of banks making medium- and long-term loans to industry. Given that the demand from industrialists for long-term loans was relatively weak – according to this consensus view – financial provision during Britain's industrial revolution was probably beneficial to industrial growth, certainly not damaging.

(ii) The middle decades of the nineteenth century

This general picture of British banks concentrating on the provision of short-term credits but, at the same time, portraying on occasions a willingness to lend long, alters little for the middle decades of the nineteenth century.

There were major structural changes within the banking sector itself but the type of business conducted does not appear to have changed dramatically. The most important structural change was the growth in the scale of operations for individual banks, a growth closely associated with the wider adoption both of the corporate form of share ownership and of branch banking (Collins, 1988a, *51–7, 64–78*). In 1826 and 1833 Parliament removed the Bank of England's monopoly of joint-stock banking, enabling English and Welsh banks to issue shares to the general public (a freedom already enjoyed in Scotland and, since 1821, in Ireland). As can be seen in Table 3.1, by 1850, 99 joint-stock banks were in business in England and Wales, managing a total of almost 600 offices; by 1875, 122 such banks were operating 1364 offices.

Ultimately the adoption of the corporate structure opened the way to the creation of massive national banks based in London, but this was to be a gradual process and for many decades the new joint-stock banks were typically small concerns whose businesses were locally based (Crick and Wadsworth, 1936, *ch. 1*). Also significant is the persistence of private partnership banking in England and Wales. The number of private banks peaked in the 1820s (Pressnell, 1956, *11*) and private partnerships continued either to lose custom to rival joint-stock banks or to become incorporated themselves by issuing shares to the public or through merger with joint-stock banks. Nevertheless, the demise of private banking in England and Wales was a long drawn out affair. As Table 3.1 shows, in 1850 there were still 327 private banks with a total of 518 offices (equivalent to 90 per cent of the number run by joint-stock banks); and in 1875 there were still 236 private banks with 595 offices (or 44 per cent of the joint-stock offices). Most of these businesses were local, often focused on rural communities.

All in all, then, during the middle decades of the nineteenth century English banking (whether conducted by the new joint-stock banks or the earlier private banks) continued to be conducted locally and on a relatively small scale; the figures from Table 3.1, for instance, mean that in 1850 each joint-stock bank was operating only six offices on average, and in 1875, an average of eleven. There were a few untypical banks managing large networks of

Table 3.1 *Number of banks and banking offices, 1825–1913*

Date	England & Wales				Scotland		Ireland		UK	
	Private banks		Joint-stock banks							
	Banks	Offices	Banks	Offices	Banks	Offices	Banks	Offices	Banks	Offices
1850	327	518	99	576	17	407	16	184	459	1685
1875	236	595	122	1364	11	921	12	440	381	3320
1900	81	358	83	4212	10	1085	10	614	184	6269
1913	29	147	41	6426	8	1248	10	789	88	8610

Sources: England and Wales: *Banking Almanac*. See Michael Collins, 'The English Banking Sector and Monetary Growth 1844–80', University of Leeds Economics Discussion Paper, No. 102 (1981), pp. 5–6; and Shizuya Nishimura, *The Decline of Inland Bills of Exchange in the London Money Market, 1855–1913* (Cambridge, 1971), pp. 80–1. Scotland: S. G. Checkland, *Scottish Banking. A History, 1695–1973* (London, 1975), pp. 424, 497, 530, 743–6. Ireland: *Banking Almanac*.

branches (e.g. the National Provincial Bank of England which in the 1840s had 90 offices throughout the country) but more representative of the new joint-stock banks were those such as Barnsley Banking Co. and the Cumberland Union Bank, with locally based head offices, a small number of branches and a business heavily dependent on the economy of the immediate vicinity.

Examination of the records of some of the early joint-stock banks has revealed that the attitude of bankers in the early nineteenth century to asset structures and industrial lending was, in essence, carried through to the mid-century, at least in the North of England (Collins and Hudson, 1979; Cottrell, 1980, *194–247 passim*). As before, the main source of funds for these bankers was deposits which were potentially subject to sudden withdrawal. Also, the greater part of their lending was still in the form of short-term credits (again, either as overdrafts or bill discounts). But, as in the earlier period, there are instances of close supportive ties with industry. Thus, local businessmen were frequently involved in establishing the new joint-stock banks and they continued to be prominent amongst the banks' directors and shareholders. And, of course, local businessmen were amongst the banks' most active borrowers. The banks also routinely provided some medium and long-term loans. These could take the form of long-term advances agreed at the outset or they could arise from the continual renewal of short-term credits. Once more, though, data deficiencies make it impossible to quantify precisely the relative importance of longer term credit from the banks to industry. One particular difficulty with drawing general conclusions for England is that, so far, even less is known about bank lending in London than in the provinces.

In Scotland the lack of legal restriction meant that both the corporate structure and the use of branch networks were well established at a much earlier date than in England and Wales. Thus, by 1850 the average Scottish bank was operating 24 offices; 84 offices by 1875 (Table 3.1). Yet, apart from the greater importance of the note issue in Scotland (where Bank of England notes were not legal tender), the overall liability and asset structure of the Scottish banks did not differ greatly from that of banks south of the border. This was certainly true of the general liquidity of loans and investments. Most loans made by Scottish banks were of a short-term nature, but (as in England) there were many instances of medium- and long-term credit being provided for the productive sectors of the economy (Munn, 1981, *193–216*; Checkland, 1975, *416–23*). This also seems to have been true of the Belfast-based Irish banks (Ollerenshaw, 1987, *94–101*).

Thus the picture that is emerging for deposit banks outside London seems fairly consistent. They were credit banks, not investment banks. Their asset structure was kept quite liquid but the granting of some long- and medium-term loans was quite normal. Also as many of these banks were relatively small and locally based (especially in England and Wales) their commercial ties with the local business community were often close. Unfortunately, when it comes to considering the central issue of whether the banks of this period were more willing to support industrial customers than those of later years, the truth is that we do not know. These provincial banks are the ones that industrial customers would have found most convenient to turn to for aid and, as has been argued, there are many examples of such aid having been granted. But the evidence compiled so far is too piecemeal to permit comparisons with a later date. And a major deficiency remains the lack of specific work on London banks and their attitude to local businesses. A more systematic research programme into bank lending is required.[3]

So far, the discussion has concentrated on the largest deposit-gathering financial institutions – on the deposit or retail banks – but what of other institutions? Were not non-bank financial intermediaries involved in industrial finance in this period? Apparently not. None of the other major financial institutions was committed to any significant degree to the promotion or provision of finance for domestic industry. The London discount houses were specialist institutions concentrating on the purchase and resale of commercial bills of exchange (Scammell, 1968). Another important group of City of London institutions, the emerging merchant banks – amongst the best-known of which were Rothschilds, Barings, and Brown, Shipley & Co. – directed their efforts to two main areas, neither of which included domestic industry. As a group they were heavily involved in providing international credit and commercial intelligence and in issuing long-term funds for overseas governments and public utilities (e.g. railways) (Chapman, 1984; Perkins, 1975). Indeed, domestic industry did not become a serious concern for any of these firms until after World War I.

Involvement by the insurance companies (whose total funds at this time were large, equal to about one-third of those of the deposit banks) seems to have been somewhat more evident if, none the less, insubstantial. During the middle years of the nineteenth century these companies did not invest in equity (or, indeed, in any of the very few non-government securities quoted on the Stock Exchange) but a growing share of their assets was held in the form of loans and mortgages to corporations, individuals and firms. Most of these funds were directed into urban development and railway construction but a small (and, unfortunately, unquantified) proportion was on loan to commercial and industrial concerns (Supple, 1970, *309–30*; Dickson, 1960, *258–63*).

Of the other formal financial institutions, building societies, friendly societies and savings banks specialised in promoting middle- and working-class thrift and, besides, the type of assets they could hold was closely circumscribed by legislation. They did not invest in, or lend to, industry.

In addition to these institutions there was a miscellaneous batch of intermediaries that industrialists may have turned to for 'outside' funds on occasions, but about which little is known. Local attorneys, financial advisers and company promoters may well have provided assistance at times. In addition, the law (especially with the reforms of 1856–61) did permit industrialists to adopt the corporate structure and to issue shares. But in fact very few did so. The great bulk of industrialists retained individual or family control over their businesses. Indeed, in the mid-nineteenth century conversion of an industrial partnership to a joint-stock company was familiar only in such leading sectors as the cotton-spinning, coal and iron and steel industries (Cottrell, 1980, *104–61*). Even here public participation was very limited, with existing partners typically retaining the bulk of the new company's shares. It is also significant that the organised stock exchanges in London and the provinces did not actively provide the funds to finance new industrial issues (Michie, 1987, *3–8*; Killick and Thomas, 1970). They did however provide a secondary market in the shares of the very few existing industrial companies.

To return to the overall picture, it seems that industrialists continued to rely mainly on their own reserves (either personal wealth or, more commonly, 'plough-back') and those of family and acquaintances for long-term finance. There are instances of some of the non-bank financial institutions providing accommodation but, in general, investment in domestic industry here was almost non-existent or, at best, peripheral. It seems more likely that if industrialists of the mid-nineteenth century should have required outside funds then they would have turned to their local bank. Public flotations of industrial concerns were costly and rare and, anyway, could involve dilution or loss of control for existing partners. A long-term loan from a bank, on the other hand, would be a natural progression arising from the operation of an account that routinely provided short-term credits. Indeed – as has been suggested – in practice medium- and long-term loans could easily arise out of the continual renewal of short-term accommodation. Moreover, while the cautious banker would probably ask for collateral and keep a close check on the transactions on a debtor's account, he/she would not normally seek any direct control over how industrial customers ran their own businesses.

4

Banks and industry, 1870–1914

As has already been emphasised, it is disquiet with the UK's economic performance from the late Victorian and Edwardian periods that has fuelled claims that there were serious deficiencies in British financial provision. Despite the continued dearth of empirical work on the pre-World War I period, historians and economists have not been deterred from making broad generalisations about the nature and extent of participation by the banks in industrial finance.

Critics claim that at this crucial time in the country's economic development – when the newly industrialised countries of Europe and North America were threatening Britain's market share and when the need for rapid adoption of more sophisticated technology and organisational structures became paramount – the banks failed industry. Two assumptions are fundamental to the critics' case, and both are debatable. The first of these is the belief that British industry would have benefited from a greater injection of capital than was actually achieved in the forty years or so before World War I – in essence, a belief that more industrial investment would have improved productivity and long-term growth. The second supposition is that it was the banks that were denying industry access to these funds. The first of these assumptions involves such broad issues – in effect, calling for a general appraisal of the actual and potential growth of the economy – that its treatment lies beyond the scope of the current study. (It should not be forgotten, though, that it is an assumption, not a fact.) Here, it is on the second assumption that we concentrate.

It is important to draw a distinction between demand and supply when considering the market for industrial finance. It has already been shown in Chapter 1 that a lack of involvement by the banks could be taken as evidence of either the absence of an active demand for funds from industry, or of an unwillingness on the part of banks to participate in the market (a supply constraint). On its own, then, 'evidence' of a lack of involvement cannot distinguish between demand and supply. If, on the other hand, historians were to uncover numerous instances of financial institutions refusing to fund 'worthy' projects that were being put forward by industrialists, then this could be accepted as strong condemnatory (if not conclusive) evidence against the banks. However, it must be said that – so far, at least – no such general direct evidence of this sort has been produced. (Harrison, 1982, gives some indication of the difficulties of raising finance faced by a company in a new technology sector – cycles, 1891–1914 – but he also illustrates the importance of bank funds to the particular company with which he was concerned.)

On the demand side, in fact, it is commonly accepted that the typical industrialist in this period did not actively seek long-term financing from financial institutions (Cairncross, 1953, *95–102*; Cottrell, 1980). Most manufacturing concerns in Britain continued to operate on a relatively small scale. Many were family-owned and family-run businesses that financed most investment requirements from accumulated profits or, if required, from funds raised from private, non-institutional sources (e.g. friends and acquaintances). Liberalisation of company law between 1856 and 1861 had facilitated and cheapened the adoption of a corporate company structure and extended limited liability to the shares of enterprises of all kinds but, even so, most firms taking advantage of the legislation formed 'private companies' – in 1913 these accounted for 80 per cent of all companies in Britain (Cairncross, 1953, 97). The main attraction of incorporation as a private company was that it enabled the partners to gain the advantages of limited liability on shares at the same time as allowing them to retain control by restricting the issue of those shares to a pre-selected group: to themselves, members of their family, personal acquaintances, and so on. For the most part, incorporation did not signal that an enterprise was seeking external funding. There were a few notable exceptions but, in general, manufacturing companies did not seek their funds on the organised capital market, and even less so in London than in the provinces (Michie, 1987).

A generally held view is that:

> The lack of development and innovation in [the provision of external capital] was primarily a reflection of the lack of demand for this type of finance, due to manufacturing industry's continuing reliance on internally generated funds. In many respects agents in the formal capital market were not called upon to provide the services of intermediation for industrial companies . . . (Cottrell, 1980, *269*)

According to this view, financial institutions were not supplying industrial funds because industry was not demanding them. Thus it could hardly have been the 'fault' of the banks if the rate of industrial investment was deficient. This, indeed, has been the retort of the banks themselves throughout the past hundred years. They have been able to claim that they have always been prepared to meet the legitimate needs of their customers (e.g. Gilbart, 1911, *vol. 2. 391*).

On the other hand, the banks' critics do not accept that their case is damaged by the absence of direct evidence of financial institutions turning away industrialists. They argue that the financial institutions' aversion to long-term loans and investments in industry was so well established by the late nineteenth century that industrialists would not have bothered to seek such funds from the banks. Nor would this reluctance to approach the banks and other institutions necessarily be based solely on the expectation that their requests for funds would be turned down. It could be that borrowing in the organised capital market was too expensive or, more insidiously, it could be that the influence of the prevailing banking ideology was so powerful that it even convinced industrialists themselves. In this view, then, the absence of bank refusals is evidence of a lack of demand from industrialists only in a secondary sense – the primary cause was the policy of non-involvement by the banks. To repeat, in practice it has been no easy task to distinguish between autonomous demand and supply factors.

The rest of this chapter and the next considers the evidence and arguments under three main heads: Deposit Banking; The Capital Market; City vs Industry (Chapter 5).

(I) Deposit banking

It is generally accepted that by the turn of the century the main deposit, or retail, banks (those which were later known as the 'clearing banks') did not provide long-term industrial finance to any significant degree. Contemporary bankers themselves emphasised the liquid nature of their assets, stressing the need to maintain public confidence in their ability to pay cash on demand. The little information from the few accounts that were published gives the same impression. The bankers' published balance sheets, on the one hand, gave no information as to the extent of their commitments on industrial loans and investments and, on the other, served to emphasise the liquidity of their portfolios.

In broad terms, this picture of liquidity-conscious banks concerned with short-term loans and safe, readily-saleable investments (such as British government securities) was confirmed by Charles Goodhart's work on the internal records of a number of the London clearing banks (Goodhart, 1972). Goodhart found that by the mid-1890s these banks believed a (historically very high) 15 per cent ratio of cash to deposits should be displayed to the public and that the ratio of 'available assets' to public liabilities should be in the region of 40–45 per cent. 'Available assets' were those considered the most easily encashable – namely, cash itself, money at call and short notice (lent to the London money market) and British government Consols. By the beginning of the new century, the varying price of Consols had led to some banks excluding them from their most liquid assets and to downgrading the significance of the 'available assets ratio'. In its place bankers looked to a ratio of liquid assets to liabilities, where 'liquid assets' were restricted to cash and money at call and short notice. It became generally accepted that the banks' balances should display to the public a liquidity ratio of some 30 per cent (Goodhart, 1972, *167–91*). Goodhart also confirmed that the London clearers did not hold British industrial securities. In other words, his research generally emphasised the banks' overriding concern for liquidity, with their concentration on the short end of the money market.

However, while Goodhart's work is one of the very few attempts at empirical analysis of the composition of bank assets and liabilities for this period, it should be acknowledged that he deals with broad categorisations (e.g. 'advances', 'investments') and he has extremely little to say directly on industrial lending. For instance, he was able to show that in the early years of the twentieth century, over 50 per cent of many of the London banks' deposits were invested in loans and overdrafts but he attempts no analysis of the liquidity and duration of loans, or of the type of borrower. Once more, detailed historical work on the relationship between banks and industry has yet to be done.

Nevertheless, the currently available evidence all points in one direction – by the beginning of the twentieth century Britain's deposit banks did not provide industry with long-term funds to any great extent. Some commentators believe that the institutional structure of British banking may have been an important part of the explanation for this deficiency.

(i) Changing structure of deposit banking

Major changes transformed the institutional structure of British deposit banking in the half-century to World War I. All parts of the UK were affected, but the transformation was most dramatic in England and Wales. In the middle decades of the nineteenth century the English retail banking system had consisted of hundreds of separate banks, the orientation of whose business was typically local. By World War I, however, the great bulk of the business was in the hands of a few London-based companies operating branch networks throughout the country (the Irish and Scottish systems were still separate). Some figures will indicate the magnitude of the change. In 1850, the average English joint-stock bank had been operating only some five branches; by 1913 there had been a 32-fold increase, with an average of 156 branches (Collins, 1988a, *521*). Similarly, public liabilities per (British) bank had risen from about £360,000 in 1850, to £4.6 million in 1900, to £11.6 million by 1913 (again, a 32-fold increase on 1850).

The increase in scale arose partly out of 'internal' growth as individual banks expanded and opened up more branch offices, but mergers between banks accounted for the most dramatic spurts in size. There were a number of 'waves' of mergers, with the peak of activity occurring in the late 1880s and early 1890s, with a total of 67 mergers between 1888 and 1894 (Capie and Rodrik-Bali, 1982). By the culmination of this process in 1920, the 'Big Five' banks (Barclays, Lloyds, Midland, National Provincial and Westminster) alone accounted for 80 per cent of English bank deposits. Elsewhere, Britain's two other banking systems, in Scotland and Ireland, were affected in a like manner. Indeed, the Scottish banking system had led the way in terms of mergers and market concentration, with the number of banks down to just ten by the 1880s (Checkland, 1975).

In themselves growth in scale and greater market concentration in banking would not necessarily be damaging to industry. In fact, a theoretical case could be made that larger, more stable and more efficient banks might improve the delivery and range of services on offer. Thus, bigger banks should have been more capable of meeting the needs of those customers in the industrial and commercial sectors whose own scale of operations was increasing on trend. Also, larger pools of deposits and a greater spread of assets should have reduced risk and, theoretically, could have induced the banks to hold more diversified portfolios, including (potentially) industrial loans and investments.

In fact, it is generally accepted that this structure did provide Britain with a stable system that was effective in providing everyday retail banking services. In contrast to many other countries, for instance, the last serious deposit bank failure in the UK was in 1878; and the sophistication of Britain's domestic chequeing and bank remittance services is acknowledged to have been unparalleled at the time. These are advantages that should not be underestimated. Within an international perspective, UK industry (along with the rest of the economy) gained significantly from the absence of the recurrent series of bank failures which continued to be an important disruptive feature of financial developments in countries such as the USA.

In other critical respects, though, the structural and institutional changes that took effect from the 1870s are said to have worked against industry. One effect was to bring about the demise of local banking, thus reducing the direct personal links between local businesses and banks that may have been an important source of industrial funds in earlier times (Best and Humphries, 1986). It is true that some important Lancashire banks (e.g. Martins, the

District and Williams Deacons) retained a strong regional base well into the twentieth century and, of course, the national banks employed local branch managers or agents, or even local directors, whose responsibility it was to keep abreast of developments in their locality. But, critics claim, the close bond between local banks and local industry which had been possible earlier in the nineteenth century, had been irrevocably broken. The emergent giant institutions had their head offices in the City of London. They were clustered around Lombard Street, close to the discount houses, Stock Exchange and Bank of England, where government finance and international intermediation were the prime concerns – far removed from domestic industry based in the Midlands and North (or, indeed, in the London environs).

Policy was being increasingly determined in the City and the creation of massive organisations from what had been numerous constituent companies made it imperative that head offices devise means of establishing a common corporate identity, internally consistent policies and centralised control (Holmes and Green, 1986, *89–119*; Sayers, 1957, *241–75*). Local managers were employees who had to follow head office directions and British banking lost much of its local initiative. The (often implicit) suggestion is that the new organisations found it easier to establish control by imposing relatively simple, standardised rules on all their managers (Cassis, 1985a). This, in turn, would have operated against risk-taking, against involvement with local industry. Then, over time, as managers were moved to new offices or retired and a new generation appointed, these national organisations lost much of the expertise in the assessment of local requests for industrial finance that had been built up by the smaller constituent banks.

The propagation of a conservative attitude to bank investments and loans was not purely internal to individual banks. It received important external endorsement as banking became a 'profession' and a body of acceptable banking practices became established. Leading bankers and other commentators extolled the importance of maintaining public confidence by holding a highly liquid asset portfolio. Standard works taught new bankers what risks were acceptable and what assets were attractive – and long-term loans and investments to the private sector were not amongst them

(Gilbart, 1911; Rae, 1888). In this way, critics claim, British retail banking as a whole became imbued with conservative attitudes towards portfolio management and minimised long-term lending to industry.

In fact, it was not just industrial lending that was affected. There are signs of a generally more conservative and restrictive approach from around the turn of the century. The figures in Table 4.1 show a marked slow-down in the growth of bank deposits by the early twentieth century. In one sense this is the expected growth path for a successful new product (bank deposits and services in this case). Initially (in the mid-nineteenth century) there was rapid growth as bank offices were opened in new areas and new customers recruited but:

by 1900 the more readily exploitable parts of the retail deposit market had already been tapped and new branches were opening up in less densely-populated and less wealthy areas, or were duplicating existing facilities operated by rival banks . . . For the future, growth of bank deposits would proceed more steadily, depending largely on the rates of population and income growth, as well as on the rate of inflation. (Collins, 1988a, *49–50*)

By the turn of the century, the retail banks had lost some of the dynamic benefits that had accompanied the earlier, heady days of rapid growth. But part of the loss was self-inflicted. There was a strong conservative streak in late Victorian and Edwardian banking practice. One aspect was a general move to restrict competition by imposing interest rate cartels (Griffiths, 1973; Checkland, 1975, *391–2, 486–7*). Another was the adherence to specialisation. As with other British financial institutions, the retail banks confined their business to a relatively narrow area. The vastness of their deposit resources suggests that the banking conglomerates of the early twentieth century could have diversified and offered a broader range of services (including industrial financing) but they did not do so. Although they became increasingly involved in the financing of international trade through expansion of their acceptance businesses, domestically they continued to concentrate on the provision of retail banking services. They did not merge as 'universal banks' offering a broad range of services. Their services were also essentially intermediary in character. Crucially, according to their critics, they declined to

Table 4.1 *Long-term growth of UK bank deposits*

| | (a) Commercial bank deposits per £100 of GNP* £ | | (b) Rate of growth of commercial bank deposits (% p.a.)* | |
			(i) At nominal prices	(ii) At constant prices
1875	42.0	1850–1875	4.7	4.0
1900	47.4	1875–1900	2.2	2.7
1913	46.2	1900–1913	1.6	1.1

* All figures used in the calculations are five-year averages centred on the dates shown, except for 1913 when an average for 1910/13 is used.
Source: (Collins, 1988a, 47–8).

take on any managerial responsibility in the provision of funds for industry – they did not become investment banks of the sort some historians believe operated in the USA and Germany (Kennedy, 1987; Tilley, 1986). It is in this regard that the supply of British banking facilities is said to have been deficient. On the other hand, as we have stressed, such arguments can be countered by drawing attention to the nature of demand for funds. Thus, an important counter-allegation that will be examined later is that the absence of investment banking in the UK was probably because there was no demand for it from British industry.

(ii) Impact of crises

One specific explanation of why the banks of the mid-nineteenth century may have become more cautious over time and less inclined towards industrial finance, centres on the effect of liquidity crises. The middle decades of the century were marked by a series of liquidity crises, in 1847, 1857, 1866 and 1878, during which note and deposit liabilities were withdrawn and the public's balances of currency (coin and Bank of England notes) were built up. During these short-lived 'panics' there was general anxiety that banks might collapse, failing to meet their obligations to pay depositors and note-holders on demand – hence the public's desire to switch to currency. To the banks, such crises emphasised how vulnerable their business was to a loss of public confidence and it has been suggested that the lesson many of them drew from the shock of the crises was that larger holdings of cash, near-cash and other liquid assets were the best means of reducing such vulnerability. In particular, there is evidence that after each of these crises the banks in England and Wales tended to maintain a higher proportion of very liquid assets, so that on trend their portfolios became more liquid (Collins, 1988b).

The crisis of 1878 has been singled out by many writers as being particularly significant for its effect on bankers' attitudes towards industrial loans (Checkland, 1975, *469–81*; Holmes and Green, 1986, *57–69*; Best and Humphries, 1986, *227–8*; Kennedy, 1976). It has been shown, for instance, that for the banks the run on liabilities in 1878 was the worst of the mid-nineteenth century (Collins, 1989). Moreover, during the crisis a number of provincial banks experienced an extremely difficult time because they had extended loans to industrial customers who, because of prolonged recession, were finding it impossible to repay in a hurry. What is more, the problem of illiquidity inherent in long-term industrial financing was openly discussed in the press at the time. The suggestion, therefore, is that after the immediate crisis had passed bankers in general were more cautious, more liquidity-conscious and less willing to lend long. In the following decades, the merger movement, the emergence of national banks and the more formal professional training of bankers provided the vehicles in which this aversion to industrial lending was spread to the whole system.

This is the argument but, once more, it must be stressed that detailed empirical work is still required before it can be generally accepted. The severity of the 1878 liquidity crisis has been established but the long-term effects on bank lending are still largely conjectural and more research is required. Besides, it is worth reiterating a point made earlier: to the extent that the British banks' cautious approach ensured a more stable banking system – with fewer instances of bank failures than overseas – domestic industry would have benefited to some degree. All commentators agree that stability brought advantages. The debate, in fact, is over the question of degree, over whether or not the bankers became unduly concerned with liquidity, became unnecessarily cautious.

(II) Structure and efficiency of British capital markets

Michael Edelstein deals explicitly with the allegations of bias and institutional rigidities – allegations of 'market failure' – within Britain's capital markets of the late nineteenth and early twentieth centuries. He has been particularly concerned to test allegations that the capital market was biased towards both overseas investment and low-risk securities. He dismisses both these allegations (Edelstein, 1982, especially *chs 1–3, 7, 13*; Edelstein, 1976).

Two aspects of his argument are directly relevant to the relationship between financial institutions and domestic industry. First, he is keen to emphasise the general competitiveness and responsiveness of the capital market to the needs both of existing and of new industrial firms, despite appearances to the contrary (especially in London). Secondly, he attempts to test statistically for bias in the market.

He accepts that the issuing houses of the first-class merchant banks based in London concentrated on good quality, large-scale business – in effect, on the flotation of large-sized issues of securities by British and overseas governments, by railroad companies and by other public utilities. In other words, they did not handle the issues of domestic industry. However, he points out that this specialisation was not irrational; it was not a reflection of conservative bias and institutional inflexibility. Instead, he argues, there were 'sound technical reasons' for specialisation. More especially, cumulative experience in a particular area of business (e.g. large-scale overseas issues) would undoubtedly have bestowed certain economies on the issuing houses. Conversely, 'since a high proportion of the limited companies in need of the service of professional issuing houses were relatively untried enterprises, it is probable that there were even diseconomies in the joint production of small and large-size security issues' (Edelstein, 1982, 52). Thus problems could have arisen if the first-class merchant banks had diversified in this manner. In particular, their commercial success depended upon accumulated expertise and upon maintaining the confidence of clients in their ability to launch successfully new issues of securities. They would have been foolish, therefore, to run the risk of the high failure rate that might accompany an excursion into any new type of business in which they had little experience – the risk of taking on smaller scale flotations could have seriously damaged their reputation and, therefore, their existing large-scale business.

Thus Edelstein is keen to establish that there was an economic rationale in the first-class merchant banks' concentration on the issuing business that they actually chose – a rationale for the absence of domestic industrial issues. He is equally keen to stress that this is not evidence of bias against domestic issues. He points out that the main issuing houses avoided *all* medium- and small-scale security issues whether they were domestic *or* foreign; there was no particular bias against domestic issues.

Edelstein also accepts that the business of the London Stock Exchange was dominated by securities issued by British and overseas governments and by domestic and overseas railroads. That is, that there was a notable absence of domestic business equity. Ranald Michie confirms this. He shows that in 1873 government securities amounted to 59 per cent of all securities quoted on the London Stock Exchange and that railroads accounted for a further 32 per cent; commercial and industrial securities totalled just 1.4 per cent (Michie, 1987, 54). Forty years later the proportions had altered – with 35 per cent in government securities, 43 per cent in railroads and under 10 per cent in commercial and industrial securities – but the relative unimportance of domestic industrials remains apparent.

Is this evidence, though, of inadequate capital-raising facilities for domestic industry? According to Edelstein and Michie it is not; it merely shows that very few industrialists sought to raise capital in the formal market. Instead, they argue, many more diverse and less formal sources of funds were available to British businesses, and it was these that were used, although they do admit that our knowledge of such sources is limited. Edelstein, for instance, points out that on occasions there were many small, often ephemeral firms that specialised in raising the relatively small amounts of long-term funds required by domestic businesses. In fact, between 1866 and 1883, 243 of all the new limited companies registered stated this as their main line of business, although Edelstein does acknowledge that, in practice, almost one-half of them had disappeared within ten years. Nevertheless, he suggests that these figures are evidence that adequate facilities were available to those British industrial firms that were seeking to raise capital. In addition to such small-scale specialists, he stresses that outside London a mixed bag of institutions, professional partnerships and individuals played a supportive role in meeting industry's requirements. Industrial firms were able to borrow short-term credit from their deposit bankers and renew this if required, and longer term funds could usually be borrowed from friends and acquaintances. If further funds were required through the issue of securities, 'at a minimum the services of a local solicitor, banker, professional stock broker or London company promoter would be purchased to handle legal formalities and the cash transactions' (Edelstein, 1982, *54*).

Although these services were often informal, Edelstein believes they were nonetheless competitive and adequate to meet the modest requirements of domestic industry. Michie agrees: 'Where the funds required were somewhat beyond the means of a single individual it was relatively easy to raise the amounts required . . .' (Michie, 1987, *105*). Edelstein is also keen to stress the importance of the provincial stock markets which traded in local industrial issues and thus increased the liquidity of local securities (regular trading on local markets facilitated disposal, purchase and redistribution of assets by provincial investors). All in all, such local facilities for raising industrial capital were normally adequate to the demand. Moreover, if a provincial firm did require funds on an unusual scale, then a London promoter could be employed. Finally, for the very biggest flotation, first-class businesses were able to employ the leading London merchant houses to organise flotations in London (as, for example, happened in the case of brewing, cotton textiles, chemicals and iron and steel).

W. A. Thomas summarises this optimistic view of pre-1914 capital market provision. 'It would appear that up until the First World War there was no significant gap in the provision of medium- to long-term funds for small firms. Industry had little difficulty in obtaining outside finance, and did so without making use of the public issue of negotiable securities' (Thomas, 1978, *116*). The general judgement of these 'optimists', then, is that the structure of the pre-1914 British capital market was appropriate to the needs of British industry and other capital users. They admit of no, or very few, institutional constraints on the supply side. Instead they emphasise that the organisation of the market, with its small number of first-class firms concentrating on large-scale issues and the myriad of small specialists and quasi-financial advisers and institutions (in both London and the provinces) was an appropriate response to the demands placed on it.

The second, and more novel, part of Edelstein's contribution to this debate is his attempt to test formally for bias in the operation of the capital markets. The two alleged biases that he examines are:

(i) The suggestion that British capital market institutions (especially merchant banks and investors) were biased in favour of overseas assets.

(ii) The claim that these same institutions and investors were biased in favour of large borrowers.

Both allegations are, of course, critical to the charge made against the financial institutions that they 'failed' industry.

Edelstein conducted his main tests on equity shares, using data for thirty-five industrial groupings over the period 1870–89, and for thirty-seven industrial groupings for the years 1890–1913. Thus two sets of results emerge, but the findings are the same in both cases. In essence (although, for simplicity, abstraction does some injustice to mathematical purity), Edelstein tested the following functional relationship:

$$\lambda = f(X, Sc)$$

where

λ is a measure of the expected rate of return from a particular asset (over and above the rate of return on a riskless asset) modified to take account of the degree of uncertainty about receiving the expected rate of return;

X is a variable denoting the national origin of an asset: 0 if the industry was domestic, 1 if non-domestic;

Sc is a variable differentiating between large-scale and small-scale issues: 0 if small-scale, 1 if large-scale.

If allegations of bias in favour of non-domestic assets are correct then the sign on X should be negative $(-)$; and if there was bias in favour of large-scale issues, the sign on Sc should also be negative $(-)$.

Table 4.2 reproduces Edelstein's results (and, for those who are interested, provides the full equation that he tested). In terms of the statistical technique employed (linear regression analysis),

Table 4.2 *UK capital market biases: regression tests*

Index of market returns utilised	X	Estimated equation: $(R_j - R_c)/Cov(R_j, r_m^i) a_1 + a_2 X + a_3 Sc + e$ Coefficient t-values for ScA	ScB	R^{-2}	# obs.
1870–1889:					
r_m^1	−0.74	insig.		0.02	37
r_m^2	−1.22	−0.61		0.05	37
1890–1913:					
r_m^1	1.68		−0.46	0.08	37
r_m^2	1.24		−0.77	0.10	37

Source: (Edelstein, 1982, *70*).

these results are uniformly poor, suggesting in themselves that his measures of bias explain very little of the behaviour of the index of market returns (λ) over these time periods. The coefficients of determination, R^{-2}, are very low and, for the technically-minded, the t-statistics are insignificant (at the 0.05 level these need to be at least 2.04 to be significant). In other words, neither the domestic/non-domestic variable (X) nor the large-scale/small-scale variable (Sc) offers any statistically significant explanation of the movements in the index of returns (λ). Edelstein interprets this as strong evidence of lack of bias in British capital markets either in favour of overseas issues or in favour of large-scale issues.

Before accepting these results at face value, though, the restrictive nature of underlying assumptions must be acknowledged. Use of Edelstein's particular formulation is based on a series of theoretical assumptions, assumptions that abstract from reality. For instance, he assumes that all investors had similar attitudes towards risk and expected returns; that they operated on similar decision horizons; that buyers and sellers of securities had access to the best information available; that the capital market was highly competitive; that arbitrage was effective and that all assets were close substitutes. In effect, Edelstein assumes perfect market conditions.

It is on this critical question of how 'perfect' (in the economist's sense) the market actually was that Edelstein has come under attack from those who stress institutional rigidity within the market. William P. Kennedy has been to the fore in dismissing Edelstein's claims (Kennedy, 1974; 1976; 1987). Central to Kennedy's case is the view that the capital and money markets were, indeed, biased and that they were highly segmented. He highlights the institutional specialisation that has already been referred to and he claims that, for example, the concentration of the merchant banks and London Stock Exchange on large, overseas, non-industrial securities did, indeed, reflect bias. Above all, British investors were risk aversive. For support, Kennedy points to the data drawn from Edelstein's earlier work (Table 4.3). According to Kennedy, the figures are clear proof of how selective British investors were, of how they avoided risky assets – proof, in other words, of bias. (Although the reader should note that the proportion of both 'risky' and 'safest' securities rises over the period.)

To counter Edelstein's faith in the market to respond positively to any demand for industrial capital, Kennedy claims that, in reality, there were serious market failures. The most serious problem was segmentation into distinct submarkets with ineffective arbitrage between them. The segments were created by supply deficiencies, by institutional specialisation and bias – with, for instance, one market for short-term credit (serviced by the retail banks), another for bills of exchange (by the discount houses), and yet another for large-scale overseas and public sector security issues (by the merchant banks) and so on. Significantly, there was no organised market (and no corresponding specialist institution) for the small- and medium-scale financing of domestic industry.

As we have seen, neither Britain's retail banks nor merchant banks showed much interest in industrial financing but according to Kennedy this was not because there was no need for it. In fact, he attempts to calculate the potential gains that were forgone by the country because of its failure to exploit new technology. He believes that these losses were substantial. According to his calculations, if Britain had been as successful in exploiting the new technology of the late nineteenth century (electricity, internal combustion engine, scientific chemistry, etc.) as she had been in exploiting the technology of the early nineteenth century, then in

Table 4.3 *Percentage distribution of outstanding home and foreign securities in the UK (by value), classified according to risk*

Class of risk	1870 (tot. = £2.3b) (%)	1913 (tot. = £7.9b) (%)
1. Safest	44	55
2. Moderate risk	37	14
3. Risky	18	31

Source: M. Edelstein, 'The Rate of Return on UK Home and Foreign Investment, 1870–1913', University of Pennsylvania, unpublished PhD thesis (1970), *253–7.*

1913 British income per capita would have been at least 50 per cent greater than actually achieved.[4] Unfortunately, Kennedy argues, the opportunity to gain such a dramatic improvement in living standards was not exploited and a large part of the reason for this failure lies in capital market deficiencies.

What explanations does Kennedy offer for the failure of financial institutions to respond to such bright prospects for commercial gain? Two basic reasons are put forward. The first of these is the persistently conservative, risk-aversive attitude of the institutions. On the whole they held 'safe' investments, characterised by the large holdings of government and public utility (often overseas) securities. When there was any involvement with British industry, the deposit banks, insurance companies, investment trust, company promoters and stockbrokers almost always restricted themselves to an intermediary role between borrower and investor. Unlike their counterparts in other countries (Germany and the USA are most frequently cited) British financial institutions shied away from taking on any managerial responsibility for the operation and development of their industrial customers. The contrast is drawn between overseas banks that encouraged technical and organisational innovation amongst their industrial debtors as a means of safeguarding their own investment and British bankers who offered an intermediary service with minimal involvement in how investment funds were to be spent. Kennedy supports his case by attempting to show how the capital market failed industrialists in three critical high-technology industries of the late nineteenth/ early twentieth centuries: electrical engineering and supply, motor vehicles, and chemicals. Britain's financial institutions performed badly compared to overseas banks and his general conclusion is that:

> capital markets in the US and Germany, by making resources available to a large group of technologically progressive industries on a scale un-equalled in Britain, account for much of the difference in the economic growth performance between these two countries and Britain (Kennedy, 1987, *120*)

For Kennedy, then, an important part of the responsibility for Britain's low rate of growth in the half-century to the First World War rests with the banks, because of their timidity and conservatism.

The second explanation Kennedy offers for capital market failure is informational imperfection. During the period the legal and institutional framework badly distorted both the effectiveness by which those seeking funds could signal their intentions and the channels through which would-be investors could obtain full and accurate information. For instance, because of institutional special-isation it was not easy (contrary to what Edelstein and Michie have assumed) for potential investors to gain access to information on profits and yields in British industry. For Kennedy there was no single, national pool of savings. Instead, there was a series of 'relatively small, highly segmented pools of savings' with no effective arbitrage between assets (another of Edelstein's essential simplifications). Part of the problem was the state of company law which enabled businesses to provide incomplete or misleading information from their accounts: 'the asymmetrical distribution of information deeply embedded in these arrangements makes it highly probable . . . that there [were] critical crippling gaps in the market channels needed to arbitrage effectively those yield differ-entials that '[were] perceived' (Kennedy, 1987, *126*).

Finally on the question of market inefficiency and bias, Kennedy dismisses most of Edelstein's statistical analysis as flawed because of the nature of the sample of securities he uses. Kennedy claims that only high-quality securities were selected and that this pre-selection inevitably excluded those very assets (belonging to medium and small-scale domestic industrial companies, especially in manufacturing) that the debate centres on. Edelstein – it should be stressed – accepts none of these criticisms and, indeed, he does not even accept the validity of Kennedy's international comparison. In particular, he denies that US banks were involved with industry in the way that Kennedy claims.

In summary, the debate is still hotly contested with a major division of opinion over whether Britain's capital market was efficient or inefficient and unbiased or biased. As has been emphasised, part of the difference of opinion arises out of the different views taken by historians of the available 'factual' information on the adequacy of informal sources of industrial capital. All are agreed that the formal market in London contributed very little to industrial capital formation in Britain. However, the nature and amount of evidence on informal sources of capital is such as to leave 'the facts' in dispute. It is possible that in this area further historical research may be able to provide a more adequate picture of what actually happened (see Michie, 1981, for an example of such research). The other major reason for the division of opinion is more philosophical, even political, and is thus much less likely to be resolved by the uncovering of further data. In essence, the division revolves around the degree of faith the various contributors have in market forces. The 'optimists' such as Edelstein and Michie believe that 'the market' (both formal and informal) responded in an appropriate manner to the demands placed on it. The critics such as Kennedy lack such faith and argue that supra-market direction of funds into industry would have markedly improved Britain's growth performance. This fundamental divide becomes more obvious in the next chapter when we consider criticisms of the role of the City.

5
City vs industry, 1870–1914

This is a series of arguments about the City's failure towards industry which transcends the narrow debate over the efficiency of economic markets. These arguments take a much broader view of British economic development by placing it within a political and sociological context. In essence, the claim has been that the interests of 'finance' as represented by 'the City' have frequently differed from those of industry. Critically, so the argument goes, in British history it has often been the financial sector that has gained the necessary economic and political influence to ensure that its interests have been safeguarded, even if these have operated to the detriment of industry.

(i) International character of British finance

An essential ingredient in the debate over the alleged conflict of interest between City and industry concerns the growing inter-nationalisation of British finance. It will be beneficial, therefore, to summarise the main features of this international perspective before considering the allegations in more detail.

During the years 1870–1914, City of London institutions were at the centre of a burgeoning system of multilateral finance. To those engaged in international transactions these institutions offered insurance remittance services, a broad range of financial advice and provided both short-term and long-term borrowing and lending facilities at internationally competitive rates. In fact, by the beginning of the twentieth century City institutions dominated the international credit system. The sterling bill (or 'bill on London') was firmly established as an extensively used means of granting international credit. Most of these bills were drawn on a select group of major merchant banks (e.g. Hambros, Rothschilds and Barings), on the London offices of overseas banks and (from early in the new century) on the main London clearing banks. In addition, the London discount houses provided a buoyant secondary market for such bills and this widely enhanced their liquidity and marketability.

City institutions also played a prominent role in the international market for long-term capital. The merchant banks were active in advising overseas governments, railroads and other public utilities on how best to raise funds in the UK. As we have already noted, some of these banks developed specialist issuing and underwriting businesses which were largely geared to overseas securities (Chapman, 1984). Operations on the London Stock Exchange also showed a strong commitment to overseas securities (Cairncross, 1953, *95–102*; Morgan and Thomas, 1962). Thus foreign securities accounted for about one-half of the value of the paid-up capital of all securities quoted on the Exchange from the 1880s up until World War I (Michie, 1987, *54*).

The importance of the international dimension to British finance is beyond doubt. What is still controversial is whether this external orientation was damaging to British industry. One strongly stated view has been that overconcern with the international sector diverted resources away from domestic industry (see Pollard, 1985; and 1989, *58–114* for a survey of the debate). A common claim, for instance, is that it was cheaper and easier for overseas governments and foreign public utilities such as railroads to raise capital in London than was the case for domestic manufacturers (e.g. Saville, 1961, *57*) and, as we have seen, there is a more general suspicion of bias within the capital market. Another aspect of the scale of the City's international business which is sometimes stressed is the fact that it bestowed on the banks a relative independence from the fortunes of domestic industry. In countries less committed to international finance the profitability of the financial sector would have depended more directly on the performance of the domestic economy. But in the UK this interdependence was less, because the banks earned more of their income from their overseas interests. So, the argument goes, there may have been less need for the banks to foster the growth of domestic industry. Indeed, this is just one facet of a much broader condemnation of the City's pernicious influence over the country's political and economic structure.

(ii) Economic liberalism and domestic industry

Many commentators argue that the conflict between banks and industry can be properly appreciated only within a broad political and social context (e.g. Ingham, 1984). They take as their starting point the general commitment – of the state, of the main political parties and the major economic institutions – to a 'liberal economic regime' throughout the second half of the nineteenth century and into the twentieth century. The three central pillars of this regime were free trade, laissez-faire and sound finance. The reforms of Huskisson, Peel and Gladstone in the middle decades of the nineteenth century had sharply reduced the restrictions on international trade in goods, and successive governments retained a free trade commitment up until the 1930s. Similarly – although there were specific digressions and despite the fact that the state (especially in the guise of local government) was, on trend, taking on more welfare responsibilities – successive governments and their advisers maintained a general faith in the efficacy of the market economy and need to minimise government interference in the operation of markets (Taylor, 1972).

One important aspect of laissez-faire was the maintenance of tight controls over government finance. In effect, minimum intervention implied minimal state expenditure (after allowing for essential services such as defence and law and order). But public sector expenditure was also governed by the general political adherence to 'sound finance'. This effectively meant that government budgets should be balanced – i.e. expenditure outlays should be adequately covered by revenue (from taxes, etc.). If this could be established as the norm then financial profligacy by 'irresponsible' governments would be constrained and the British government's credit safeguarded. In fact, the concept of 'sound finance' reached beyond the confines of state budgets and embraced the forms of monetary and exchange rate regimes adopted by the country. For the UK, this meant a commitment to the international gold standard and to an anti-inflationary monetary policy.

In all, then, the nineteenth-century commitment to this liberal, or neo-classical, economic regime ensured the maintenance of free trade, minimised state economic activity and upheld sound finance. As we shall see, the argument of the critics (though not all individuals agree on every particular point) is that whereas such a regime may have been appropriate in the mid-nineteenth century when Britain enjoyed industrial hegemony on world markets, it became less so over time. More international competition, the increasing complexity of technology and the trend towards larger scale production, meant British industry's requirements changed. Thus, it is sometimes argued that by the end of the nineteenth century when other industrial nations were increasingly restricting international competition, tariff protection might have been beneficial to some British industries. So, too, could have been the emergence of 'agencies' (whether in the guise of the state or the banks themselves) to undertake the necessary risks and provide the long-term capital essential for industrial rejuvenation. But such changes did not occur, policy remained committed to economic liberalism. As a result, according to the critics, British industry suffered.

The present survey must be confined to the monetary aspects of this broad debate. Below, there is first an assessment of the operation of monetary policy in the period, then a consideration of the debate as to the nature of the City's political and economic influence.

(iii) Monetary policy

The legislative and administrative arrangements governing Britain's pre-1914 monetary regime embodied the twin principles of sound money and an open economy. During the French Wars (1793–1815) the government had suspended the legal obligation on banks to pay gold on demand in exchange for their notes (at the time most banks throughout the country issued notes, the major exception being the London area where the Bank of England's notes enjoyed a monopoly). Subsequently, however, wartime inflation and depreciation of the international value of the pound were seen by many as serious problems and a number of influential commentators came to believe that these were the direct result of note inconvertibility which had allowed the banks 'to print money' (Fetter, 1965). Soon after the war had finished, therefore, two acts of Parliament (passed in 1816 and 1819) prepared the way for the country's return to the gold standard. Under the gold standard the value of the currency (the pound sterling) was fixed in terms of gold, with all bank notes convertible to gold (if only indirectly through Bank of England notes which became legal tender in England and Wales in 1833). The Acts of 1816 and 1819 allowed for a gradual resumption of specie payments – by May 1823 at the latest – with the ultimate adoption of the Mint price of £3 17s. 10d. (£3.89) per standard ounce of gold (in fact, the Bank of England adopted convertibility before the deadline, from February 1821). The international character of the standard was ensured by allowing the melting down of coin and the unrestricted export and import of bullion and specie.

The basic legislative framework of the nineteenth-century gold standard was completed by the passing of the Bank Charter Act of 1844. The main objective of this act was to control closely the note-issuing powers of the country's biggest issuer, the Bank of England. It did this by forcing the Bank to hold a full, 100 per cent, specie reserve against all notes issued beyond a permitted fiduciary issue (which was originally set at some £14 million). Under these new arrangements, 'the Bank not only had to maintain full convertibility but also had to alter its note issue – £ for £ – only in line with changes in its gold reserve' (Collins, 1988a, *125*).

Contemporaries believed that these legislative arrangements would closely circumscribe the power of banks – and, indeed, of the state – to create money. In particular, supporters of the gold standard hoped they would minimise the dangers of inflation inherent in an unfettered system of inconvertible notes.

The restrictive nature of the gold standard, in its effects on monetary policy and possible consequences for the domestic economy and British industry, can best be illustrated through Bank of England action. The Bank of England's position was pivotal to the country's monetary system and (in the absence of state action) it was the one institution with responsibility for whatever monetary policy there was in the period. It was the government's own bank, it was the principal note issuer, many other monetary institutions kept part of their cash balances on deposit at the Bank and it was the main repository of the country's monetary reserve of gold (the commercial banks kept their own holdings of coins to a minimum). As a result Bank of England decisions on such matters as its willingness to lend to other institutions and on the rate of interest to charge on such loans, could have important consequences for the wider economy.

The Bank's obligations under the gold standard are critical to understanding its evolution as a central bank (Collins, 1988a, *178–92*). As it was the main repository of the nation's gold reserve it was inevitable that significant changes in the exchange rate would force the Bank to take action which, in turn, could – in fact, was intended to – affect the rest of the monetary system. Thus, if world demand for sterling fell relative to other currencies (e.g. because Britain was exporting less/importing more, or because more capital funds were flowing overseas from Britain than were coming in) *ceteris paribus*, this would cause a depreciation in the *market* value of sterling. Under the gold standard, however, the extent of such a fall was extremely limited because of the authorities' commitment to convertibility at the *official* or *par* rate (i.e. £3.89 per ounce of gold in 1821). As holders of sterling (in the form of legal tender notes or claims on notes) saw its market value begin to fall below the official rate, then they would go to the Bank of England (via their own banks) to convert their paper sterling to gold at the official rate – there would be little sense in accepting the lower market rate.

The effect on the Bank of England would be to reduce its reserves (as it paid out gold for notes). Legal obligation meant the Bank had no choice but to pay out gold on demand yet, at the same time, this legal obligation also meant that the drain on the Bank's gold could not be allowed to continue unchecked. Obviously, beyond a certain point further reductions in the reserve would undermine the public's confidence in the Bank's ability to pay gold on demand. In practice the bank began to take remedial action long before this critical point was reached, but the legal framework necessarily constrained the form this action could take. By definition the commitment to the gold standard ruled out currency devaluation (i.e. reducing the official exchange rate between gold and sterling) or the suspension of cash payments. The Bank had to devise other means of alleviating the pressure for gold.

By the late nineteenth century the main technique developed by the Bank was the use of short-term interest rate changes, which were made effective by the use of open market operations (Sayers, 1957; 1976). Typically, in the face of adverse exchange rate movements the Bank would increase the rate of interest charged on its loans to the money market (especially 'Bank rate' charged on bill discounts) and it would ensure that the institutions within the market (conventionally, the discount houses) were obliged to borrow at this new higher rate by mopping up spare liquidity through the sale of some of its massive holdings of securities. In a simplified form, the sequence was that the Bank would raise the interest charge on loans to the discount houses and sell securities (at a reduced price) to money market institutions. In turn, these institutions, in order to buy the extra securities, would run down their liquid balances including those held with the discount houses (Scammell, 1968). The discount houses, in consequence, would be forced to replenish their diminished resources by borrowing at the Bank of England at the new rate of interest. Ultimately, the discount houses, banks and other financial institutions would have to cover the higher cost of acquiring funds by passing on the higher rate of interest to their own customers.

An effective Bank rate policy of this sort could thus influence general market conditions, pushing up interest rate when the exchange rate and the Bank's reserves were threatened. If working well, the rise in rates made the purchase of British securities relatively more attractive on international markets, increasing the demand for sterling, offsetting the initial deterioration in its value and easing the drain on the gold reserve (Bordo, 1984).

It must be emphasised that, at the time, Bank officials devised this method of reacting to gold flows out of a relatively narrow concern over how best to meet their legal obligations. They did not see themselves as operating 'monetary policy' as we would understand it today:

over the period as a whole the Bank did not accept or adhere explicitly to

[a] quantity theory of money. In its central banking function, the Bank was more narrowly concerned about the impact of gold flows on its own reserves rather than about the state of the balance of payments, the general level of prices, movements in the money supply, or other national economic indicators. (Collins, 1988a, *181*)

In support of the Bank it should be acknowledged that on occasions it did use (admittedly, marginal) discretion in its reaction to gold flows (e.g. its occasional variation during the two decades prior to World War I of the terms on which gold could be imported – the so-called 'gold devices') rather than relying solely on automatic reactions to external pressures. The Bank also contributed significantly to the stability of the British banking system through its preparedness to operate as a lender of last resort in liquidity pressures. The frequency of bank failures in the UK was much less than in many other countries and this must have been of great benefit to industry along with other sectors of the economy. Also, to the extent that the Bank's successful management of the gold standard enhanced the international status of the City – by helping to avoid devaluation for nigh on a century, by minimising the impact of liquidity crises and by encouraging the use of sterling as the world's leading currency – it made a positive contribution to the City's invisible earnings on the balance of payments.

However, it is for its broader representation of City interests that the Bank has been attacked (Harris and Thane, 1984; Ingham, 1984). Within this context critics claim it was the Bank that became a major instrument through which the Establishment's concern for external stability 'damaged' the domestic economy. The nature of this damage, at least for the pre-1914 years, is not always spelt out, however. For instance, there have been no serious studies as to whether UK industry would have benefited from sterling devaluation around the turn of the century; and it must be acknowledged, of course, that maintenance of the gold standard ruled out currency appreciation as well as depreciation. Similarly, while it may be legitimate to point out that the operation of Bank policy (higher interest rates, etc.) may have had a deleterious, deflationary impact on the domestic economy when the gold reserve was under threat, this needs to be balanced by the recognition that an appreciating exchange rate would normally lead to lower interest rates at home. As is often the case within the debate over banks and industry, there has not yet been sufficiently detailed empirical research either to accept or to refute many of the allegations.

But the critics' case against the Bank of England is drawn much more broadly than any narrow concentration on 'measuring' the impact of Bank action. To these critics the Bank is seen as the champion of the City and that alone is damning. Obviously, within such a broad condemnation, drawing attention to the niceties of policy technique or channels of monetary transmission is largely beside the point. To the critics, it was the thrust of policy *in toto* which is said to have damaged industrial prospects. The Bank's importance as a government adviser and initiator of policy is readily acknowledged. What is condemned is its neglect of the industrial interest. Within the Bank's management there was close personal identification with the City – Bank directors were either merchants or merchant bankers (Cassis, 1985b). It is claimed that, in effect, the Bank's actions were assessed only with respect to financial yardsticks and the interests of overseas trade – would a particular action be good for the pound, good for the City? It certainly did not use its immense influence or vast resources to direct funds towards industrial investment. The nineteenth-century policy paradigm in which the Bank operated was moulded by financial and commercial interests, not those of industry. It is in this sense that Bank of England influence has been condemned.

(iv) Reasons for the dominance of the financial interest

If the operation of monetary and exchange rate policy were as damaging to industry's interests as the critics of the City suggest, why was the financial interest able to gain control over the most important political and economic decision-making agencies and to retain control over such a long period? At first sight, such dominance during the nineteenth century seems ironic for this was, taking the long view, when British producers had been so successful in leading the developed world on the path to industrialisation. Why did the growing band of influential industrialists not take control themselves?

We have already noted in Chapter 2 that the historical division between the industrial and financial interests in Britain and the apparent inability of industrialists to attain a superior (or even parallel) political position has been the source of much debate over the applicability of a Marxist schema of capitalist development. At the beginning of the twentieth century Hilferding and Lenin had forecast the eventual merging of both 'interests' as the common concerns of the British capitalist class became apparent with the loss of industrial hegemony (Hilferding, 1910, translation 1981; Lenin, 1969 reprint). At the same time, Hilferding offered possible reasons for the continuation of the divide amongst Britain's capitalists: Britain's early industrial lead had reduced industrialists' need for outside capital from the banks (as Gerschenkron was to emphasise much later), large overseas earnings gave British financial institutions a certain independence from domestic industry and the involvement of City institutions in promoting the international economy added to the conflict of interests. All three 'explanations' have featured prominently in more recent contributions.

Frank Longstreth, for example, argues that within the dominant capitalist class, specific politico-economic 'fractions' can be identified, fractions whose interests may well conflict (Longstreth, 1975). There was such conflict, for instance, in the struggle between landed and commercial interests over the Corn Laws. Since the late nineteenth century, though, Longstreth claims that the dominant fraction within the British capitalist class has been 'banking capital', or City interest, which has successfully secured control of the leading organs of economic policy, particularly the Bank of England and the Treasury. As we have seen, the Bank's role was central to the conduct of monetary and exchange rate policy and Longstreth believes its effectiveness in fostering the fortunes of the banking interest helped 'institutionalise' the City's political dominance. 'The City has . . . largely set the parameters of economic policy and its interests have generally predominated since the late nineteenth century' (Longstreth, 1975, *162*). In contrast, 'industrial capital' has remained surprisingly weak and its opposition to policies that could damage its own interests has been muted.

Even though Longstreth intends that his analysis should apply to

Britain from at least the late nineteenth century, he concentrates on the post-1918 years and thus does not give any specific examples of how the City's political and social dominance may have damaged industrial interests prior to World War I. Once again, we are left to speculate as to whether the commitments to the gold standard, to sound money and to free trade were contrary to the interests of British industry.

W. D. Rubinstein and Geoffrey Ingham are two more writers who discuss the debate over banks and industry within a broad sociological and political context (although both are at pains to reject various aspects of Marxist analysis). Significant for our purposes, they also deal more fully with the nineteenth century than writers such as Longstreth. Both Rubinstein and Ingham accept that there was a major conflict of interests between the financial and industrial sectors – a conflict which transcended mere economic issues, one which went to the core of British politics and society. However, there are major points of departure from Longstreth's analysis.

An important part of Rubinstein's work has been concerned with estimating the distribution of wealth amongst the very wealthy and in assessing the implications this carried for political and social elites during the nineteenth century (Rubinstein, 1976; 1977; 1986). His major finding is that, despite the industrial revolution and despite continued industrial growth throughout the century, the share of industrialists amongst the very wealthy was surprisingly small. Landowners remained the numerically largest group of 'very wealthy' but even amongst the non-agricultural sectors, merchants and bankers were much more prominent than manufacturers. Moreover, there was a strong geographical bias in wealth distribution. Manufacturing tended to be located in the provinces (the Midlands and the North) whereas commerce and finance were concentrated in the South-East, especially in the City of London (although some provincial entrepots such as Liverpool and Edinburgh enjoyed local concentrations of professional services). As manufacturers tended to be less wealthy than merchants and bankers, the consequence of this occupational divide was that the national distribution of wealth was skewed towards the City even at the height of Britain's industrial hegemony. Indeed, Rubinstein claims that data on income distribution suggest a similar type of distribution for middle-income groups as well.

Moreover, Rubinstein posits that there was a serious social, economic and political rift between the wealthy bankers of the City and the less wealthy manufacturers of the provinces. At a basic level, the City was independent of domestic industry for its income because, as we have seen, much of this came from international and government finance. Therefore, the City's economic objectives were different (with its commitment to the international economy, to a stable exchange rate, etc.). In addition, a social and religious rift existed. Provincial manufacturers were often nonconformists, the City was mainly Anglican. A career in a bank was also more acceptable to the powerful aristocracy than a lifetime spent running a factory. Thus the personal and social bonds between finance and land were much greater and this added to the political strength of the banking interest *vis à vis* the industrial interest (Cain and Hopkins, 1987). Finally, the political and social influence of the commercial and banking elite was secured by its willingness to send its sons to the major public schools, to university at Oxford and Cambridge, and so permeate the highest echelons of the British Establishment – gaining a readier access to political influence in government and the civil service than was possible for the industrial elite of the provinces (Cassis, 1985b).

Rubinstein leaves no doubt that this deep dichotomy within Britain's elite was severely damaging to industry:

The role of the City during the nineteenth century was of course largely to finance foreign and government loans, and it did not act as a capital market for British industry until the very end of the century. British industry in this period was self-financed or financed by local banks whose directors had few City connections. This was . . . of the utmost importance to Britain's economic development and it has been a major factor in the chronic under-investment of British industry. (Rubinstein, 1977, *116*).

Geoffrey Ingham's historical analysis parallels that of Rubinstein in many respects although he takes exception both to the latter's loyalty to a Marxist schema and to important aspects of Rubinstein's chronology (Ingham, 1984). But Ingham's contribution can be more readily appreciated by highlighting his points of difference with Longstreth. There are three main bones of contention. First,

Ingham rejects the concept of 'fractions' within the capitalist class, mainly because they are too difficult to identify. Secondly, he argues that Longstreth (and Rubinstein) underestimate the role of the state in that they follow other Marxist analysts in arguing that the dominant economic group is able to 'capture' control of the machinery of state and use it for its own ends. In contrast, Ingham argues that the two institutions responsible for the formulation of economic policy (the Bank of England and the Treasury) played an important *autonomous* role in promoting policy that was conducive to City interests. They did this not as 'tools' of the banking fraction but because it suited their own interests to do so. Thus in the case of the Bank of England, by the late nineteenth century its own prestige and influence owed much to its ability to maintain the gold standard – loss of the gold standard would weaken its own position. Similarly, the Treasury's power base lay in its role within the bureaucratic machinery as the arbiter of sound budgetary policy. In other words, according to Ingham, once established, institutional self-interest ensured that these agencies became powerful, independent defenders of policies central to the City's political hegemony.

The third and most important of Ingham's departures from the views of Marxist writers is his view that the City's activities were essentially commercial in character. As Kennedy does in another context, Ingham stresses that City institutions concentrated on their role as intermediaries rather than principals in the provision of both short- and long-term capital. It was thus in their interests to operate as open an economy as possible to promote the free movement of goods, money and capital. They had no direct interest in the production of goods, rather they offered their services as middlemen and in this regard overseas customers were as welcome as domestic firms. Ingham also reiterates many of the points we have already discussed concerning the City's lack of involvement with domestic industry. In general, he agrees with the view of critics such as the institutionalists that this lack of involvement created a major constraint on the supply of funds to industry: 'It is not . . . too sweeping a judgement to say that . . . the City stood in complete indifference (and, in all probability, ignorance) of domestic industry' (Ingham, 1984, *150*).

Although this chapter has considered a variety of opinions

critical of the City's role, all these agree on the paramount importance of supra-market influences – on the importance of social, political, as well as economic forces. To these critics, the operation of financial markets cannot be properly analysed without giving due consideration to the society in which such markets operated. In reality, it is argued, it was these broader influences that set the parameters to the performance of economic markets and institutions; and in the British case between 1870 and 1914, the influence of 'the City' operated against that of industry. Indeed, as will become clear in the next chapter, some commentators claim that this fundamental conflict between finance and industry has persisted into the twentieth century and, in many ways, was brought more sharply into focus after World War I when Britain's place in the international economy was inexorably altered.

6
The interwar period

World War I (1914–18) was followed by a sharp, short-lived boom which collapsed in 1921. The British economy then entered a troubled phase which was to last through the next two decades. The outstanding economic problem of these years was the chronic contraction suffered by the export trades: in constant price terms, exports during the 1920s averaged just four-fifths of the immediate pre-war level and in the 1930s only two-thirds of that level (as a proportion of Gross Domestic Product, exports fell sharply from 24 per cent in 1913, to 21 per cent in 1929 and down further to 15 per cent in 1937). This collapse in exports was closely associated with the second major economic characteristic of this period, mass unemployment. National unemployment averaged 9.1 per cent of total employees (12.8 per cent of insured workers) during the 1920s and 12.8 per cent (16.5 per cent of the insured) during the 1930s but, as many of the export industries were geographically localised (e.g. Lancashire cotton textiles and South Wales coal), some regions of the country suffered much worse unemployment rates over a prolonged period. Whereas a number of important industrial sectors did experience reasonable growth in the period – especially those industries able to meet growing domestic demand and those able to exploit new technology and markets (e.g. motor vehicles and electricity) – the problems of lost exports and unemployment remained essentially problems of industry.

The common perception amongst modern commentators is that there was a fundamental need both for improvements in industrial productivity – with the more rapid adoption of new technology and working practices – and of organisational changes within industries (e.g. mergers and closure of inefficient plant) and for a general restructuring of Britain's industrial base. For this period, restructuring could only mean switching resources (labour and capital) from those sectors that had lost markets (the export sectors) to sectors with expanding (home) markets. This type of factor transfer is, of course, occurring all the time in modern economies but the peculiarity of the interwar years was the large scale of structural change required and the fact that it had to be achieved against the background of a very sharp contraction in world markets, especially after 1929.

A growing number of influential contemporaries argued that essential industrial restructuring would be greatly facilitated if Britain's financial institutions could be persuaded to adopt a radically different approach to the financing of industry. In effect, they called upon the banks to employ more of their vast resources for the good of the country by financing industrial investment, by encouraging industrial customers to 'rationalise' their production methods (Foxwell, 1917; Clay, 1929, *186–9*; Thomas, 1931).

A closer degree of cooperation between the banks and industry could well be expected during this prolonged period of economic dislocation. From industry's point of view, the need for outside funds would probably be that much greater – struggling firms facing contracting markets would need financial support while they coped with the fall in sales receipts and loss of profits; and innovators would require additional capital if they were to re-organise. Circumstances would also have put pressure on the banks themselves to become more involved. At the micro-level, the prolonged nature of the problem facing some industrial customers meant that they would have had difficulty repaying loans and the banks would be drawn more deeply into the commercial affairs of these customers in order to protect their own commitments. More broadly, there could be mounting pressure for a general realignment of industrial and financial institutions. From a Marxist perspective it could be argued that the damage to the British industrial base was such as to threaten the whole capitalist system, including the prosperity of the City. On the face of it, if a fusion of the financial and industrial interests of the sort envisaged by Hilferding and Lenin is to have any validity in British economic history, surely it would have occurred between the wars when the economic foundations of the whole capitalist class seemed under threat? It is just this sort of argument, in fact, that writers such as W. D. Rubinstein and John Foster employ to claim that the various sections of the British capitalist class did, indeed, find much more common ground after World War I than in earlier periods (Rubinstein, 1976, *116*, *125*; Foster, 1976, *10–12*). However, it is not necessary to invoke a Marxist schema to imagine that the City and industry could have been drawn (or pushed!) more closely together as the multilateral trading system and international gold standard first began to crumble and then collapsed in the 1930s. Undoubtedly, the international economy was much less buoyant after World War I and (especially after 1929) the incomes of many City institutions were badly hit (Clarke, 1976, *15–16*, *103–4*; Chapman, 1984, *101–3*). The City thus lost some of its economic independence from the domestic economy and may have become more involved in the affairs of domestic producers.

However, a different interpretation is stressed by another group of commentators. These concede that the banks made some moves towards providing more funds for industry (or made borrowing easier) but that the basic conflict between financial and industrial interests remained. Indeed, the nature of the conflict became more apparent in the 1920s and 1930s when British industry's international vulnerability was seriously exposed for the first time. These critics emphasise that the scale of industrial disruption, loss of markets and unemployment called for drastic remedial action – not marginal adjustment – but it was here that the response of Britain's financial institutions was found seriously wanting. As we shall see, some writers suggest that this tardiness was the result of institutional rigidities which left the banks unwilling or unable to respond adequately to the needs of industry (Tolliday, 1987; Best and Humphries, 1986). Yet another group of writers stresses the continuance of broad socio-political factors, arguing that financial interests retained their political grip over policy; and their traditional commitment to a liberal, non-interventionist, imperialist (and, in the 1920s, free trade) stance was to prove non-conducive to British industrial restructuring and rejuvenation (Ingham, 1984, *170–99*; Longstreth, 1979, *157–73*; Overbeek, 1980, *99–107*).

As for previous periods, historians of the interwar years have thus been concerned to establish not only the extent but also the qualitative nature of any bridging of the divide between finance and industry. Once again, the search has embraced both the operations of financial markets and the formation of monetary policy.

(I) Financial markets

A. (i) *The provision of industrial finance by the banks*

As for the nineteenth century an underlying issue in the debate over the provision of funds for industry revolves around the possibility of prolonged malfunction in the money and capital markets. Is it feasible that financial institutions would continually fail to provide services if there were a demand for them? Some commentators are more inclined to believe in the efficacy of markets than others, but for the interwar years discussion of possible market failure has not been as explicit as that between Edelstein and Kennedy for the pre-1914 period. Nevertheless, it is important to acknowledge that implicit assumptions about the performance of markets underlie most judgements as to whether the banks failed British industry between the wars.

An important division of opinion which is explicit is that between those who emphasise the greater degree of commitment by the banks to industry and those who, while acknowledging that the banks were 'involved' to a greater degree, nevertheless stress the inadequacy of the bankers' response. In other words, there is general agreement that compared to the immediate pre-war years the banks played a more active role in financing industry. The disagreement arises over how best to judge this greater involvement – whether to stress the discontinuity with the minimal involvement of the past or to stress the essential continuity of inadequate financial provision.

Differences of opinion arise partly out of the nature of the data. Occasionally industrial case studies deal with the financial needs of industrial companies involved, but not always (e.g. Supple, 1977). Also available are more general data on the composition of bank assets, including loans. Nevertheless, serious gaps exist and research must continue if a fuller picture of 'the facts' is to emerge. Even then, the data in themselves will not settle the question as to the 'adequacy' or 'effectiveness' of bank provision. This is much more judgemental and, as for the nineteenth century, the different prior expectations and the different criteria employed by different historians account for most of the division of opinion. A fundamental question in this regard concerns whether or not it is reasonable to expect a commercial bank to be the dynamic agent responsible for promoting and financing industrial reconstruction of the sort required between the wars. It could be argued that such a role more rightly belongs to the industrialist (with his/her specialised knowledge and direct involvement) or, if pressure from an 'outside' agent is required, to the state (with its broader responsibilities to the economy as a whole). Why should private sector banks be expected to acquire industrial expertise and take out-of-the-ordinary risks? More critical still, why should they be expected to have any particular talent: first in perceiving the need for industrial reconstruction (especially on an industry-wide or economy-wide basis) and then in being able to implement it in an effective manner?

An individual historian's or economist's answer to these questions will fundamentally colour her/his judgement on whether the banks failed industry – and, of course, they will also colour the reader's own view.

(ii) The clearing banks' overall position

Although there were significant shifts of magnitude, the nature of deposit bank business remained essentially the same after World War I. These banks operated extensive networks of high-street branches that channelled together millions of individual retail balances into massive pools of financial resources upon which the banks drew to make their loans and investments. The nineteenth-century system of local banking had gone and had been replaced by a system dominated by a small number of national conglomerates. The 'Big Five' banks of Barclays, Lloyds, Midland, National Provincial and the Westminster dominated the domestic banking sector in England and Wales and even the 'second order' of English banks consisted of sizeable regional banks such as Martins and the District. Already by 1921 the largest eleven banks had over

£1.9 billion in deposits, operated some 7500 branches and employed 50,000 people. Individual banks had massive deposits at their disposal and although balances on individual accounts could fluctuate, the number of accounts was so great – and the spread across different sectors of the economy so wide – that, in aggregate, bank deposits were instilled with a degree of stability unknown to the local banks of fifty years earlier. Nevertheless, the clearing banks' views towards liquidity, towards the desirability of certain forms of lending and investment, remained curious and conservative.

A popular textbook of the 1930s reflected the continued concerns to retain the public's confidence: 'To earn profits at all the bankers must maintain confidence, to satisfy depositors' claims a bank must be able to convert its assets into cash *quickly*' (Sayers, 1938, *213*). This stress on liquidity directly influenced policy on loans and investments to the private sector, of course. To quote another well-known book written at the end of the period:

Modern bankers have learnt their lessons from the past, and have formulated certain principles: flexibility, liquidity, adequate distribution of risks, inadvisability of lending long while deposits are repayable on demand or at short notice, and the maintenance of adequate reserves for bad debts directly they appear to be doubtful. (Ellinger, 1940, *143–4*)

In order of 'liquidity' (i.e. of ease of sale with least risk of capital loss) the clearing banks' main grouping of assets in this period were: cash, money at call and short notice (interbank balances, on loan to the discounts houses mainly), bills (predominantly public sector Treasury bills), investments (overwhelmingly British government securities) and advances. 'Advances' were fixed period loans and overdrafts made to the private sector and, as such, were not marketable and were therefore illiquid. It is for this reason that 'sound' banks were supposed to take special care in determining their lending programmes. Walter Leaf, chairman of Westminster Bank, reflected the conservative, cautious approach adopted by interwar bankers, at least in public:

[Advances] should be running only for a limited time, with provision for reduction at least, if not full repayment, in . . . months rather than years. It is a cardinal point of sound English banking that there must be no 'lockup' of capital . . . It is not the business of the banks to supply fixed capital to their customers. (Leaf, 1926, *157*)

In other words, the clearing banks' public position was that it was not their role to supply long-term funds for industry, it was not considered a legitimate function of the deposit banks. This view was accepted by the major enquiry into banking in the period (Macmillan, 1931, *Report*, *172–3*) and it has been recently endorsed by a historian of the capital market, W. A. Thomas (Thomas, 1978, *ch. 3*). Thomas echoes the bankers' own arguments that they were retail banks that had to pay particular regard to liquidity. Therefore, the great bulk of their loans should have been for short periods. For him, it would be quite unreasonable to have expected them to make long-term investments in British industry.

Such strictures, of course, still permitted the banks to continue with their traditional role as suppliers of short-term credit to industry. In fact, the bankers of the period were extremely keen to deflect criticism by emphasising just how supportive they were of their industrial customers. Available data on bank loans go some way to confirm this view. A parliamentary enquiry into finance and industry was set up under the chairmanship of Lord Macmillan in 1929 and it reported in 1931. The enquiry collected evidence from interested contemporaries (bankers, economists, industrialists, etc.) and prompted the London clearing banks to produce data which had hitherto been unavailable to public scrutiny. One directly relevant series is that produced in Table 6.1 distinguishing the main sectors in the economy to which the banks made advances. In all, from about 40–55 per cent of advances were made to trade and industry (depending precisely upon which groups are included) although the ratio did vary from one bank to the next. The argument of contemporary bankers was that these data indicated their high degree of commitment to the industrial sector (Macmillan, 1931, *Minutes of Evidence*). Indeed, they emphasised their own passivity in the face of changing demand for loans; in effect, they claimed they were prepared to meet all legitimate demands for credit from industrial (and other) customers within the established guidelines governing the granting of such loans.

Table 6.1 *Classification of London clearing bank advances by industrial sector, 1929 and 1937*

	Percentage share of total advances	
	1929* (10 banks)	1937** (11 banks)
1. Textiles (cotton, wool, silk, linen, jute)	8.3	4.6
2. Heavy industries (iron, steel, engineering and shipbuilding)	6.4	5.2
3. Agriculture and fishing	6.9	6.3
4. Mining and quarrying (including coal)	3.0	1.6
5. Food, drink and tobacco	6.4	3.4
6. Leather, rubber and chemicals	2.2	1.6
7. Shipping and transport (including railways)	2.5	2.1
8. Building trades	4.8	7.1
9. Miscellaneous trades (including retail trades)	14.9	14.4
Total trade and industry	55.9	46.3
10. Local government authorities and public utility companies (excluding railways)	5.3	5.6
11. Amusements, clubs, churches, charities, etc.	2.7	4.6
12. Financial (including banks and discount houses, stock exchange and building societies)	14.4	12.3
13. Other advances	22.1	31.2
Total advances (£millions):	987.7	961.0

*Various dates from 22 Oct. 1929 to 19 Mar. 1930.
**Various dates from 4 Aug. to 16 Oct. 1937.
Source: (Balogh, 1947, *83*).

It is possible, however, to take a much less sanguine view of the changes affecting loans to industry in this period. Table 6.2 gives a general breakdown of the distribution of London clearing bank assets. Before the Macmillan Committee the bankers claimed that they aimed to lend some 50–60 per cent of deposits in the form of advances (loans and overdrafts) yet, as the figures show, at best they managed only to attain even the lower end of the target for a short period and that normally they were well below target. In particular, the trend during the 1930s was for a contraction in bank advances. On the figures in Table 6.2, for instance, total advances were down from an average of £959 million in 1928/30 to £914 million in 1936/38, with the ratio of advances to deposits falling sharply from 52 to 41.2 per cent. Moreover, as can be seen from Table 6.1, during the 1930s industry and commerce were responsible for a diminished proportion of even this smaller total of advances. Such a contraction is somewhat surprising not only because of the banks' declared 50–60 per cent target but because the economy experienced strong recovery in the five years to 1937. Obviously, in aggregate terms, this economic growth was not being financed by clearing bank advances (Balogh, 1947, *74–81*).

In fact, the most significant overall change in bank assets in the period was the sharp relative decline in financial provision for the private sector (including industry). Increasingly the clearers became intermediaries between private sector savings (in the form of bank deposits) and public sector debt. The full extent of the commitment to the public sector becomes apparent from Table 6.2 if the bank's holdings of 'investments' (in effect, government securities) are lumped together with 'bills discounted' (overwhelmingly Treasury bills and, therefore, short-term government debt), 'cash' (which is also a form of public sector debt) and the high proportion of 'money at call and short notice' which was indirectly used to buy government debt. In this way, by the late 1930s over one-half the banks' total deposits were committed to the public sector (Johnson, 1951). Total government debt had increased dramatically as a result of World War I when the banks had been larger purchasers, and shifts in debt management partly explain subsequent changes in the composition of bank assets (Nevin, 1955; Howson, 1988). During the 1930s government funding operations successfully took advantage of prevailing low interest rates and significantly altered the composition of debt away from short-term to longer term securities. Thus, in 1930/1 some 32 per cent of the National Debt was held in securities with over 25 years' maturity, but this had risen to 40 per cent by 1938/9. It was the subsequent greater supply of government securities which partly explains the increase in the banks' holdings of 'investments'. Perhaps to some degree public sector demands on the banking sector 'crowded out' private sector provision.

However, it has been argued elsewhere that the oligopoly power

Table 6.2 *Distribution of London clearing bank assets* (ratio to total deposits, percentage)*

Date** (end of year)	Cash	Money at call and short notice	Bill dis- counted	Invest- ments	Advances (Total value)
1923–25	12.2	6.9	15.0	18.7	48.4 (£822m)
1928–30	11.2	8.2	14.7	14.4	52.0 (£959m)
1936–38	10.6	7.4	12.9	27.7	41.2 (£914m)

*Excluding the District Bank throughout.
**Three-year averages centred on business cycle peaks.
Source: London clearing bank monthly returns, available in Forrest Capie and Michael Collins, *The Interwar British Economy: A Statistical Abstract* (Manchester, 1983), *92–9.*

exercised by the banks themselves was a significant factor in imposing supply constraints on advances to the private sector (Collins, 1988a, *chs 7, 8*). In this view, the retail banks exhibited a predominantly unenterprising competitive attitude. Despite structural changes to the markets they confined their businesses to traditional areas and, as a consequence, their relative importance in total financial provision declined as other non-bank financial institutions such as building societies and insurance funds expanded more rapidly (Sheppard, 1971). They were loyal adherents to the established pattern of demarcation in British financial markets, whereby each group of specialists (discount houses, building societies, etc.) provided a limited range of services. Despite their massive resources the clearing banks' interest in expanding into new areas such as mortgage financing or industrial investment was muted.

Of direct relevance to the decline in advances was the use the retail banks made of oligopoly power to suppress price competition. The merger movement had resulted in a small number of large banks dominating retail banking provision in England and Wales – in Scotland, too, there was a similar situation although the high degree of market concentration had been attained much earlier – and banks in both countries overtly practised price-fixing. In fact, their interest rate cartels were operated with official approval from compliant authorities at the Bank of England and Treasury, and they remained effective throughout the period (indeed, they were not abandoned until 1971). In the case of advances, the clearers set a minimum interest rate of 5 per cent for 'prime' customers (although there was some marginal flexibility for prized accounts). But during the 1930s when market rates fell, this cartel rate became uncompetitive and the banks lost business. Of particular relevance is the claim that large numbers of bond holders, including industrial firms, were induced by the lower market rates to sell off securities (whose value had risen as interest rates fell) (Nevin, 1955, *250–1*). This, too, reduced the demand for bank loans. In aggregate the fall in market rates and the fixity in the banks' rate charges would have encouraged the private sector to seek funds from outside the clearing bank sector.

A few sentences will suffice to summarise the retail banks' overall position *vis à vis* industry. Despite committing an impressively high proportion of their total advances to trade and industry the bankers in this period continued to emphasise their traditional role as suppliers of short-term credit. Moreover, during the interwar years as a whole the clearing banks became less important as providers of funds to the private sector in general and to commerce and industry in particular. In the 1930s especially, bank advances stagnated. They made good this shortfall in assets by increasing their holdings of public debt. Thus despite the widely perceived need for a greater commitment to British industry the overall picture suggests, if anything, that the reverse happened. However, as the next section will show, consideration of the detailed response by the banks to individual industrial customers raises the possibility that there may yet be evidence of a significant *qualitative* shift in the banks' practices.

(iii) Specific instances of deeper industrial financing

Despite the clearing banks' declared position on industrial financing in general there were instances in the period when the retail banks seem to have gone much further in helping industrial customers than their public utterances would suggest possible. Is this evidence of a greater coalescence between the industrial and financial interests in Britain?

The authors of a recent history of the largest of the clearers in the period, the Midland Bank, believe it is (Holmes and Green, 1986, *ch. 7*). They show the Midland becoming involved to an exceptional extent in the detailed affairs of a number of their largest industrial customers as these companies struggled with the collapse of markets and the need to cut costs. Holmes and Green argue that, at the time, the necessity to maintain confidentiality made it difficult for the banks to answer their critics publicly but, 'in private the banks could refute these criticisms by counting the cost of support for industrial customers . . . There was no shortage of examples of intervention and reconstruction' (Holmes and Green, 1986, *179*).

One of the major 'rescue attempts' with which the Midland Bank was deeply involved was that of restructuring the Royal Mail group between 1931 and 1936 (Green and Moss, 1982). This group of major shipping companies (including the Royal Mail Steam Packet Co., Elder Dempster & Co., Pacific Steam Navigation Co. and the Oceanic Steam Navigation Co., or White Star) constituted about 15 per cent of the UK's total merchant fleet capacity at the time and had important interests in shipbuilding (including Harland and Wolff, Belfast) and steel (Colville & Sons of Scotland). By 1929 the group faced collapse with gross liabilities of £120 million. The debt was so large and the consequences of failure for shipping and shipbuilding so dreaded by the City, that most of the English, Scottish and Irish banks, as well as the Bank of England, were at some time drawn into the tortuous negotiations over rescheduling the group's debt. Government guarantees of some £7 million of bank loans to the Royal Mail group also meant that the Treasury was directly involved. As almost £3.5 million of these loans had been granted by the Midland and its affiliate company, the Belfast Bank, this particular bank had more interest than most in the outcome of the affair and one of the Midland's managing directors, Frederick Hyde, devoted a great deal of his time to the detailed negotiations. After five years of complicated arrangements the group was eventually restructured, with the central shipping and shipbuilding activities remaining intact, if severely pruned.

A similar crisis affected the Scottish heavy engineering and steel giant, Beardmore (Hume and Moss, 1979, *ch. 7*). Here a desperate battle to avoid liquidation was fought out between 1929 and 1938.

In the event it was successful but only after much of the group's manufacturing capacity (in ship repairs, marine engines, locomotives, diesel engines and commercial vehicles) had been dispensed with. Three deposit banks (Lloyds, the National Bank of Scotland and the Royal Bank of Scotland) were large creditors and their patience was essential for the successful implementation of any reorganisation scheme. Subsequently these banks took a large holding of preference shares (with a par value of £1.4 million) in the group. However, for the most part the banks were reluctant participants in the rescue attempt, being largely concerned to safeguard their own interests, and they were not averse to threatening liquidation proceedings if they felt that the security of their own commitments was being put in jeopardy. Hume and Moss also claim that the banks showed no enthusiasm for the details of industrial reorganisation and rationalisation that the group had embarked upon. Such diffidence from the commercial bankers is also revealed in their dealings with the steel company, Colvilles, which was an important component of the Royal Mail group (Payne, 1979, *151–2*). In fact, the positive contribution from the banking interest came mainly from the Bank of England whose governor, Montague Norman, personally initiated many of the attempts at cost-cutting rationalisation.

The Bank of England's excursion into industrial reorganisation began in the 1920s in response to the problems of one of its own industrial customers, but culminated in the 1930s in a more broadly drawn series of initiatives which, in aggregate, constituted a marked break with the traditions of central banking in the UK (Sayers, 1976, *ch. 15, 546–51*).

The Newcastle-based firm of Armstrong, Whitworth and Co. was an armaments manufacturer which ran into serious financial difficulties after the collapse of the post-war boom in the 1920s. The Bank of England was a major creditor on the company's ordinary bank account (held at the Newcastle branch) and was drawn into a long series of attempts at reorganising and salvaging the business. This not only involved extraordinary financial provision (eventually the Bank lost 'millions' on the account) but, ultimately, it also led to the Bank taking up a controlling interest in the company's shares and to the Bank appointing outside experts to advise on overall managerial strategy.

A more general problem than that of a single (if large) customer enmeshed the Bank of England in plans to reorganise the whole Lancashire cotton industry. Loss of overseas markets meant that this industry was in serious difficulties throughout the 1920s and 1930s. Montague Norman recognised the desperate need for a scheme to cut back productive capacity to a point commensurate with the low level of demand. It was inevitable that some firms would go out of business and factories close. The governor was also extremely anxious over the position of a number of the deposit banks who were deeply involved with the cotton industry (including, but not only, those such as Williams Deacons and the District whose businesses were concentrated in the North-West of England). These banks had advanced large sums during the optimistic months of the post-war boom and now that markets had contracted so sharply they were left with a growing amount of bad and doubtful debts. The darkest days were in the Great Depression of the early 1930s when world trade collapsed. Lack of positive action would have meant continued bankruptcies in the industry and, at its worst from a central banker's perspective, might have brought down one or more banks and thus have threatened the liquidity of the whole banking system. In these circumstances, Norman felt central bank intervention was fully justified. The outcome was the establishment in 1931 of the Lancashire Cotton Corporation whose brief was to reduce capacity and reorganise the hundreds of small firms involved. The Bank of England not only pressurised the commercial banks to agree to the financial arrangements necessary to pay for the reorganisation, but also directly made loans (of £920,000) available to the Corporation, guaranteed interest payments on the Corporation's debentures and bought up the Corporation's poorly subscribed stock when it was first issued in the depths of the depression in 1931. Involvement in industrial reorganisation of this sort represented a radical break with anything the Bank had undertaken prior to World War I.

The crisis facing Britain's export sector between the wars was so serious, however, that the Bank of England also became involved in plans for a Lancashire Steel Corporation (again, as a vehicle for industrial rationalisation) and in the Royal Mail and Beardmore reorganisations. There were also to be important instances during the late 1930s of managerial intervention in three separate cases of extraordinary capital provision for steel companies (for the building of an electric steel works at Jarrow in 1938, for the continued support, also in 1938, of Richard Thomas & Co.'s integrated steel plant at Ebbw Vale, and for the completion of John Summers & Sons' strip mill in 1939).

In 1929 the Bank of England had brought together all its industrial interests under the management of a wholly owned subsidiary, the Securities Management Trust Ltd. 'The new company had only nominal capital, but it was to be the channel through which the Bank itself could provide funds for the schemes supported by the Bank. As a separate entity S.M.T. was only a body of experts advising [the Bank] on industrial reorganisation; it was not a trading body' (Sayers, 1976, *325*). The Bank also initiated and participated in the Bankers' Industrial Development Company (established 1930). The intention here was to provide capital for worthy projects submitted by the industrialists themselves for reorganising their own basic industries. It had a nominal capital of £6 million, a quarter subscribed by the Bank of England and the rest by a consortium of clearing banks and a number of other major financial institutions. Initially, the company was set up for five years as a temporary measure to deal with the extraordinary economic crisis facing the country, but two extensions meant it was not eventually liquidated until 1945. The Bank was also to become involved to a carefully controlled extent in the special provision of funds for small firms in areas of high unemployment. During the 1930s there were to be other financial initiatives, with City institutions themselves establishing separate companies to provide medium- and long-term capital for medium-sized industrial companies, but assessment of these will be postponed until the next section, on the capital market.

All in all, it is possible on the basis of the above evidence to make out a case that the banking sector was indeed more active in meeting the financial needs of industrial customers between the wars. And a number of other important instances can be quoted in support: for example, Lloyds Bank's help to the Rover motor car company (Foreman-Peck, 1981), and to the steel firm of Stewarts and Lloyds in the construction of its new Corby plant (Truptil, 1936, *105*) and the Midland's support for the Austin motor company (Church, 1979, *55–67*). In part, it also appears that the banking sector took upon itself some managerial responsibility for the direction in which the businesses of individual customers should have been moving. On the other hand, there seems little doubt that the enthusiasm for reorganising industry was much stronger at the Bank of England than at the commercial banks. Indeed, it might well be thought that this extraordinary central bank involvement was only necessary *because* the commercial banks themselves failed to take the initiative.

In fact, a recent assessment by Steven Tolliday argues strongly that the instances of bank involvement in industrial rescue attempts – in an apparently deeper financial commitment to the industrial sector – did not represent any radical break in the traditional attitudes and approaches of British bankers (Tolliday, 1987). Tolliday has conducted a case study of the banks' involvement with one of the most troubled industrial sectors, steel, and he remains highly sceptical of claims of a fundamental shift in the relationship between banks and industry. In fact, he believes that attempts at industrial intervention by the banks – indeed, by the state – were 'clumsy and ill-directed' (Tolliday, 1987, *170*). He accepts that the banks became more committed to industry in the sense that they had extended their advances to industrial customers in the euphoric boom conditions immediately following the war and that the subsequent problems of Britain's export staples meant that the banks were drawn into a greater consideration of their customers' difficulties in order to protect these loans. However, their response was diffident, relying upon the application of traditional banking values, even in the unusual conditions prevailing at the time. He stresses that the banks in this period were essentially 'powerful creditors ... rarely controlling partners' (Tolliday, 1987, *179*). They were prepared to nurse their industrial accounts and reluctantly extend credit if necessary in order to avoid their customers going under, but the 'arm's length' approach to reorganising their customers' businesses was retained and when the industrial sector began to recover in the middle and late 1930s, the banks reduced their level of commitment. The approach of the clearing banks was thus dominated by the need for them to protect their own interests (e.g. in acquiring more secure claims to customers' assets in the event of liquidation). Involvement in plans for restructuring a company to place it on a sounder commercial basis was of secondary importance and undertaken only with the greatest reluctance.

Tolliday suggests two specific reasons for the banks' reluctance to embark on industrial management even in circumstances where they had a dominant financial interest. The first was the fear of competition, because it was thought too much interference could lead to a dissatisfied industrial company moving its accounts to another bank. The second of Tolliday's specific reasons was the absence of the necessary expertise or machinery within the banks themselves for the effective assessment and implementation of restructuring programmes. More generally, though, Tolliday stresses the institutional inertia that was a crucial feature of the relationship between banks and industry in Britain. Traditionally, industry was largely self-financing and the banks concentrated on the provision of credit, with a strong resistance to taking up not only equity but any long-term industrial securities. Although this traditional mode of conducting business came under strain during the 1920s and 1930s, to Tolliday it nevertheless remained largely intact, with the banks persisting in their 'arms-length' approach to industrial customers.

Other writers support this view of the deposit banks' narrow concern with safeguarding their own positions, of their reluctance to adopt a broader responsibility for industrial restructuring (Sayers, 1976, *320*; Kirby, 1974; Bamberg, 1988). Peter Payne, for instance, has argued that whereas heavy debts made the steel companies formally the 'prisoners of the financiers', in reality the banks were reluctant to force through any radical reconstruction of this industry (Payne, 1979, *226–7*). Even one of the studies that is strongly sympathetic towards the clearing banks in the predicament in which they found themselves nevertheless confirms the picture of industrial inexperience and reluctance to adopt managerial responsibilities. Thus it is argued that, if necessary, the Midland Bank would renegotiate financial arrangements or even appoint independent assessors for advice, but generally the bank believed reform of the industrial structure had to come from the industrialists themselves (Holmes and Green, 1986, *ch. 7*). It was not the responsibility of the banks.

Tolliday, in fact, believes that the bankers' entanglements with the ailing export industries probably served to reinforce their prejudices against long-term commitments, to reinforce their stress on the liquidity of assets. One consequence was that banking profits suffered and induced greater caution (Capie, 1988; Winton, 1982, *ch. 4*). The experience of the country's biggest bank can again be used to illustrate the sort of pressure the banks came under in these years. In 1932 the Midland Bank had to provide £0.75 million to cover bad debts and another £4.8 million for doubtful debts (in aggregate equivalent to some 3.25 per cent of total advances), with most problems associated with customers in textiles, coal, iron and steel and commodities. The response of this market leader for the rest of the decade was 'markedly more cautious and inward-looking' (Holmes and Green, 1987, *190*). Another recent contribution to the debate, from Best and Humphries, emphasises this sort of evidence to argue that the banks' lending policies altered only marginally. They see it as an essentially passive response to the problems of their clients when what was needed was a positive commitment of bank resources to restructuring the country's industrial base. They conclude 'that it was in its inability to become a dynamic force in the reorganization of basic industry that, in comparative and relative terms, the British financial system "failed"' (Best and Humphries, 1986, *237*).

However, all such talk of failure in the interwar years must be tempered by the gains derived from the stability of the country's banking system. In many other countries – including the USA and Germany whose banks are so often held up as exemplars for the British to imitate – there were serious bank failures and major liquidity crises. In Britain, commercial bank caution and the implementation of an active central bank policy by the Bank of England avoided such trauma.

B. *The capital market*

The interwar years saw a reorientation of the organised capital market towards domestic industry and away from overseas issues but, despite this, British industry continued to rely upon other sources for most of its capital (Thomas, 1978, *chs 1–5*). W. A. Thomas talks of a 'marked contrast' between the new issue market of 1911–13, when 34 per cent of total borrowing went to home industries, and the mid-1930s, when over one-half of the total went to domestic industry. This switch was the result of two complementary forces: the decline in overseas business and the increased demand from domestic industry. In turn, the former reflected both a fall-off in the demand for British capital resulting from the slow-down in the world economy and the continued application by the British authorities of a (partial) embargo on overseas issues that had first been imposed because of the war (Aitken, 1970). The increased demand for capital from British industry was part reflection of the trend amongst established family firms to 'go public' through the issue and sale of securities on the market (Hannah, 1976, *61–78*). W. A. Thomas suggests that the following specific factors were also significant but does not attempt to assess their relative importance:

In terms of the demand for market capital it seems to be generally accepted that the traditional pre-war sources of local private finance were greatly depleted, while company savings in one industry were not made generally available to new undertakings in that or other industries. Also, the industries seeking capital were moving nearer to the London market. Further, there was an increase in the optimum size of firms due to technical progress. On the supply side it is possible to point to the growing institutionalization of savings associated with investment and unit trusts, insurance companies and pension funds, while investors themselves, drawing on the demonstration effect of the war, increasingly preferred a paper claim which was marketable. The growing burden of death duties also increased the desire to keep capital in a liquid form. The level of post-war taxation may also have led to a redistribution away from rich savers, thus reducing this source of personal sector savings to the market. (Thomas, 1978, *25*).

Activity on the new issues market was characterised by two booms in 1918–20 and 1927–9, each of which was followed by some years of collapse; stagnation during the Great Depression; and a very slow recovery until activity quickened for a short while in the mid-1930s. Over the period as a whole capital was raised by a wide range of industries, although the relative importance of particular sectors varied across time. During the 1918–20 boom manufacturing, heavy industry and miscellaneous sectors accounted for about two-thirds of home industrial issues. It was during this boom that a number of the established industries took the opportunity to recapitalise, the most notorious case being the cotton textile industry where wildly optimistic over-subscription burdened the industry with excessive capital and productive capacity throughout the following two decades (Bamberg, 1988). In contrast, during the peak of new issue activity in the late 1920s it was the service sector that was most prominent. Here, again, most of the issues were made by existing businesses even though a sizeable proportion came from new companies (although these suffered the most severe collapse once the boom had passed).

W. A. Thomas accepts that there were imperfections within the market during these years, especially the problems investors had in acquiring reliable information on the potential earning power of would-be borrowers. Nevertheless, his overall judgement on the performance of the new issue market is favourable:

> the market helped to provide much-needed capital for expanding productive capacity, and for short-term debt, and it did so not only for large companies but over the period for a growing number of small companies who found that they could not grow without becoming public companies. (Thomas, 1978, *34*)

According to Thomas, companies launched securities on to the market in this period either through 'public issue' or through 'offer for sale'. In the former case, the securities were offered directly to the public at a fixed price, with the company employing underwriters to ensure against failure. 'Offer for sale' was popular amongst the large issuing houses in the 1930s when they used it for domestic industrial issues. Here, the issuing house bought the whole issue from the company and then sold it, in turn, to the public. In this period the issuing houses adopted the role of principal underwriters but spread the risk amongst many sub-underwriters (such as insurance companies, pension funds and others). In fact, the general issuing and underwriting business was conducted by a wide range of financial institutions. These included finance houses, such as British Shareholders Trust, the London and Yorkshire Trust and the Scottish Finance Co. Ltd. A second group of agencies were the syndicates formed by company promoters in order to carry out particular issues. These were a mixed bag. Depending on the size and quality of business involved, syndicates could comprise little-known firms and individuals, ephemeral in nature and of varying abilities and expertise. Many stockbrokers also participated in the activities of the new issue market to some degree although a very small number (eight or so) accounted for the great bulk of issuing business done by such firms. Finally, the first-class merchant banks which had established a large overseas business before World War I participated in domestic issues to an increasing extent between the wars. Such firms as Barings, Rothschilds, Hambros, Lazards and Morgan, Grenfell found their overseas business contracting and this created an incentive to consider domestic issues. However, lack of appropriate expertise and the need to maintain their reputations meant that they would handle only the largest issues and only the most prestigious domestic companies. They never handled the issues of new, untried companies and they completely failed to meet the needs of even the best medium- and small-sized firms. Indeed, for the great bulk of industrial issues the market was bereft of financial institutions of any standing with the necessary specialism and expertise to advise and inform the investing public (Macmillan, 1931, *Report*, *167–9*). In fact, for the typical domestic issue investors had to rely upon the financial press or the advice of their brokers, while companies seeking funds had to take their chances with the miscellany of small agencies prepared to handle the issue.

The difficulties facing small-scale borrowers in the new issue market were part of the reason for the 'Macmillan Gap' that so exercised the minds of many interested contemporaries. One of the few positive recommendations from the Macmillan Committee for altering City practice was a call for some special provision for relatively small domestic issues, of between around £50,000 and £200,000 (Macmillan, 1931, *Report*, *173–4*). City institutions were reluctant to handle such issues and even where they were prepared to do so, the fixed element in handling, administration and publicity charges meant issuing costs were proportionately, often prohibitively, high. Whereas medium-sized companies might perhaps find it possible to raise capital cheaply in the provinces (Thomas, 1973, *261–2*) they were nonetheless at a disadvantage compared to large companies (which could appeal to a broad section of the investing public) or even to much smaller firms (whose bankers could often meet most of their requirements for 'outside' funds). On the one hand, the capital requirements of medium-sized firms could well be beyond the facilities afforded by the local branch bank or private individual, solicitor, etc. On the other hand, interest from the public in a securities issue would be minimal because of the inherent liquidity problems for the investor – such issues would be too small to permit an active market in those securities (indeed, they were very unlikely to be quoted on the Stock Market) making it difficult for the investor either to raise loans on them or to resell. The Macmillan Committee accepted that a serious deficiency existed and suggested that the City should consider some special provision for the small- and medium-sized firm.

The City did respond positively but the general view is that its initiatives were overcautious and their impact very limited. The main response came in the form of new institutions, especially three which were founded in the mid-1930s: Charterhouse Industrial Development Co. Ltd (established 1934), Credit for Industry (1934) and Leadenhall Securities Incorporation (1935). CIDC was financed jointly by Charterhouse Investment Trust, the Prudential Assurance Co., Lloyds Bank and the Midland. Credit for Industry was a subsidiary of the finance company, United Dominion Trust, which in turn had close relations with the Bank of England. Finally, Leadenhall Securities Corporation was the creation of the merchant bankers, Schroeder & Co. In each case the amount of capital committed was small and the vetting criteria rigorous. In the event, there were to be numerous applications but exceedingly few were successful. All three provided funds only to existing companies with a proven commercial record, though LSI and CIDC were prepared to invest in their clients' company (Credit for Industry's business was confined to making advances). Applicants had to provide undoubted security and the general aim was to nurse small but successful companies up to the point where they could 'go public'. These criteria meant that very few benefited. For instance, whereas CIDC had apparently vetted over 7000 applications by 1940, it had financed just seventeen (Holmes and Green, 1986, *183*)! Similarly by mid-1939 Credit for Industry's net loans amounted to less than £400,000 (Balogh, 1947, *302*). It is clear that: 'Much of the potential demand for capital from small businesses remained unsatisfied', the new institutions 'did not in the main tackle the problem of finding a home for unquoted issues' (Thomas, 1978, *121*).

(II) Monetary policy: the City vs industry?

There is an extensive literature on the formulation, techniques and effects of changes in monetary policy between the wars, but for present purposes it is sufficient to be selective, concentrating on what the operation of policy reveals of the relationship between industry and finance. In the period, the most apparent source of conflict between the interests of industry and monetary policy formulation revolves around the decision to return to the gold standard in 1925. It is on this decision that the discussion will be focused.

The main legal requirements governing Britain's maintenance of the gold standard had initially been suspended because of the war but the problems associated with demobilisation persuaded the government to extend the suspension into peacetime. However, early preparation for the return of sterling to the gold standard meant that government fiscal and interest rate policies were generally contractionary during the early 1920s, and in April 1925 the decision was taken to return to a gold pound at the same pre-war exchange rate of £1:$(US)4.86.

The decision was contentious in the 1920s and, if anything, it has grown more so with the passage of time. The friction arises out of the generally accepted view that the parity of £1:$4.86 over-valued sterling (Redmond, 1984). Critics argue that given that British manufacturers were already in a poor competitive position, that overseas markets had been lost and that unemployment rates were very high, overvaluation of the currency (making British goods and services dearer to foreigners and imports cheaper to Britons) was palpably damaging to industry, to the industrial labour force and thus to the British economy as a whole. Over-valuation in 1925 is condemned for restricting British international sales still further, thus weakening the balance of payments and putting pressure on the Bank of England to maintain interest rates at a higher level (and domestic monetary conditions tighter) than would otherwise have been the case. In fact, there has been much debate as to the economic consequences of the return to gold and of the significance of any subsequent overvaluation (Moggridge, 1972; Dimsdale, 1981; Matthews, 1986). However, what are more directly relevant here are 'the motives' for the decision because it is in these that the potential conflict of interest between British industry and finance is revealed.

Sidney Pollard argues strongly that the decision of 1925 was proof of the City's continuing hegemony in matters of economic policy (Pollard, 1970). He emphasises that on matters of exchange rate policy government relied upon Bank of England advice and that the Bank, in turn, reflected City prejudices. The business interests of most City institutions – and of most directors of the Bank of England – were closely bound up with international trade and finance and, not surprisingly, the City placed a high premium on re-establishing world prosperity after the disruptions of wartime. A stable and fully valued pound was seen as an essential step in the process of rehabilitation if the City of London was to regain its place as the world's foremost financial centre. Before the war the profits of these financial institutions had been heavily dependent on the maintenance of sterling as an international key currency and devaluation could undermine confidence and threaten the chances of a successful return to the pre-war system, threatening the restoration of City profits. By the mid-1920s, therefore, the City strongly favoured restoration of the gold pound at the old international parity. Pollard accepts that in proffering advice to government, Bank officials 'would not consciously favour their own pockets at the expense of the nation, but it was only human to assume that they would tend to believe that those policies were in the national interest which also happened to be in their own' (Pollard, 1970, *25*).

Critics, thus, portray the 1925 decision as a victory for the City. They also stress that the cost of this success was borne most heavily by industry and the labour force. As the leading economist, J. M. Keynes, argued at the time, it placed the burden of adjustment for the loss of international competitiveness upon the domestic economy through the general deflationary pressures of a tight monetary and fiscal policy which were an inevitable accompaniment to an overvalued currency (Keynes, 1931).

Many others have portrayed the 1925 decision as a conflict

between the interests of finance and industry. The City wanted a strong pound; industry wanted to avoid overvaluation, preferring to seek a solution within tariff-protected Empire markets (Overbeek, 1980). However, although the complaints of industry were aired with increasing urgency as the effects of overvaluation began to bite in the late 1920s, opposition from this quarter was rather muted (especially prior to the 1925 decision itself) and ineffective (Hume, 1963). Part of the explanation lies in long-established political tradition. The UK had been continuously on the gold standard since 1821, suspension had arisen only because of the extraordinary strictures created by war, and a return to gold was seen as a return to the norm. Besides, the fact that the Bank of England had been given virtually complete responsibility for operating exchange rate policy for a century or so – that governments did not claim any discretionary powers in this regard – meant that industrialists and others 'believed in the competence of the City and the Bank on the questions of monetary policy, and they do not seem to have been fully aware of the latter's effect on either international trade or domestic activity' (Longstreth, 1979, *166*). It is not surprising, then, that industrial opposition was so weak.

In fact, Geoffrey Ingham argues that the political forces marshalled against industry (and labour) were overwhelming (Ingham, 1984, *170–87*). He believes that the 1925 decision represented not only victory for the City but also victory for the autonomous power of the two main bureaucratic organs responsible for economic policy, the Bank of England and the Treasury. Suspension of the gold standard and inflation during and immediately after the war had weakened the power of these two agencies within the policy-making machinery of state. Restoration of the gold standard would not only re-establish the Bank's traditional role but it would also strengthen the political influence of the Treasury. Treasury power lay partly in its ability to impose strict budgetary limits on the spending of other departments of state and the tighter budgetary stance that would be necessary for the restoration of the gold standard would thus enhance Treasury influence. Ingham summarises his case:

There is no doubt that the City, Bank and Treasury were in accord in wanting to reconstruct the prewar liberal system, and that the Bank and Treasury ultimately served the City's avowed 'interests', but the strength of the force for the return to gold lay in the independent practices of both Bank and Treasury. The Bank's pre-eminence in the monetary and banking system stemmed from its discretionary management of the gold standard and the Treasury's political dominance within the state system was, in part, based upon its ability to apply stringent budgetary controls within the external constraint of the gold standard regime. In short, the restoration of gold was not only believed to be in the best interests of the City, but was also seen as the means by which the Bank and the Treasury could reassume their former power. (Ingham, 1984, *173*).

Finally, Ingham stresses that the political arguments in favour of a return to pre-war gold parity became overwhelming because of the coalescence of ruling elite interests that such a return represented. In particular, return to a largely non-discretionary gold standard would weaken the power of future (especially Labour Party) governments to increase expenditure on welfare benefits, subsidies and the like. Thus the decision to return won wide support from the ruling capitalist elite, even in cases where there was little or no specific economic gain.

R. S. Sayers portrays the Bank of England's position – and, by implication, the general support given for a return to gold – in a much more sympathetic light (Sayers, 1960; 1976, *110–52*). In his view, the Bank was seeking a return to the pre-war conditions not only because it was under such conditions that the City of London and sterling had been dominant but also because it was then that British trade had flourished. The Bank recognised that unemployment was largely associated with the loss of export markets. There was therefore a need to recapture those markets and restoration of the pre-war international monetary order was considered by the Bank to be a critical prerequisite. According to Sayers the Bank's objectives were positive and general, not narrow and self-interested:

[Policy] was inspired throughout by the desire to establish and maintain an international monetary system that would facilitate the revival of international trade and international investment. It was through these that the Bank saw its major chance of promoting economic health and prosperity at home: sceptical of its powers to make much impact on internal economic conditions, the Bank shared in the general view that the roots of trouble were in the great export trades, and held that it could and should help these by promoting world conditions propitious for their revival . . . the men of 1919 believed that the best monetary system was that of 1913: a world gold standard centred on London, with the Bank of England controlling the system. (Sayers, 1976, *110–11*).

Sayers' study of Bank of England records in this period also reveals that the Bank was much more sensitive to the unemployment problem in the use of its interest rate policy after 1925 than some critics have suggested (Sayers, 1976). He also details the involvement of the Bank in the various attempts to reorganise major sections of the iron and steel, cotton, heavy engineering and shipbuilding industries which were outlined in the early part of this chapter. In Sayers' view, therefore, the Bank was not a self-interested wielder of privileged power. Certainly the directors were drawn from a narrow socio-economic group but they were aware of the problems facing British industry and believed they were acting in the best interests of the country.

Thus there remain serious differences of interpretation over the motives of policy-makers and advisers who determined policy in 1925. Most observers believe that overvaluation of the pound did damage the domestic economy to some degree. In this sense the City's influence over policy is generally seen as being detrimental to industry. However, judgement as to the degree of altruism or narrow self-interest exhibited by policy-makers depends on the broad socio-political context in which it is analysed, and it is here that major differences of opinion persist.

Conclusion

In 1931 an international run on the pound forced the authorities to suspend the gold standard once more (near-full convertibility was not successfully restored until many years later, in 1958). Part of the reaction to this crisis was a break with Britain's traditional free trade policy and the introduction of tariffs on many imports (although in another important area, budgetary policy, orthodoxy persisted). There is almost complete unanimity that these decisions represented a weakening of City interests *vis à vis* industry but critics argue that British financial interests, nevertheless, retained most of their close links with the policy-making machinery of the state. In particular, the Bank of England remained the chief source of advice to ministers on monetary and exchange rate matters.. Nonetheless, the need for greater discretion in this sphere of policy meant that politicians and the Treasury were taking on greater responsibility – and, of course, the Bank itself was to be national-ised in 1946. Even so, critics of the City maintain that British financial interests suffered only a temporary set-back and that they were able to re-establish their hegemony over economic policy in the post-World War II years (Longstreth, 1979; Eatwell, 1982; Ingham, 1984). In support, they cite the evidence we have already discussed which suggests that there was no critical change in the manner in which banks provided industrial finance – indeed that the banks' involvement seems to have diminished with recovery – 'reflecting the fact that [it] had only grown in the first place because of the inability of financially pressed companies to pay off their overdrafts or loans during the slump and not as a result of a consciously developed change of policy' (Longstreth, 1979, *171*). The interwar years do not appear to have experienced the emer-gence of finance capital of the sort that some traditional Marxists had predicted; the divide between banks and industry was great enough for it to remain a contentious issue long after World War II.

7
Summary

The determination of growth rates is a major concern of modern economics and, not surprisingly, the issues involved are extremely complex. To the extent that Britain's growth has been poor (the subject of a separate debate in itself), modern economic and social history warns that it would be naive to expect to identify a simple cause or set of causes. The controversy surrounding the role and effectiveness of financial institutions highlights this point.

For the pre-World War I period anxiety over whether or not British financial institutions were facilitating or inhibiting industrial investment revolves around a widely canvassed (though contested) view that *actual* British growth from the late nineteenth century was significantly below *capacity* growth. In particular, many believe that a substantially higher aggregate rate of investment and/or a marked redistribution of investment towards higher productivity sectors was possible but, in reality, neither was achieved. As has been shown, the historical record does suggest that the most important of the formal money and capital market institutions did not provide domestic industry with a substantial amount of long-term funds. It has been possible, therefore, to claim that British commercial banks, merchant banks and the Stock Exchange contributed very little to the investment needs of all but the largest of Britain's industrial companies. Indeed, to a large extent there is general agreement that British industry obtained little of its long-term financial needs from financial institutions. More controversial and uncertain, though, is whether these institutions could, or should, have made a bigger contribution.

For those commentators who stress the efficacy of market forces, the absence of substantial institutional involvement is an indication of the lack of demand for such involvement – industrial companies generated much of their investment funds internally and, for the typical firm, any additional funds could be met more than adequately from the varied miscellany of agents available at the time. Very rarely did industrial firms require the services of the major financial institutions; according to this view, this is the reason they were not involved. The critics, of course, have less faith in market forces and claim that the absence of involvement is evidence of supply constraints, of institutional rigidities, of market failure. Moreover, there has been a significantly broader onslaught on the political influence of bankers amongst the economic elite of Britain. It is alleged that the commitment of this elite to an open, liberal economy with free trade, fixed exchange rates and sound money, worked strongly against the interests of British industry.

For many, the proof of this came after World War I. After the war, Britain's major industrial staples suffered serious losses in overseas markets, with mass unemployment as a consequence. Many commentators have suggested that industry's interests lay in currency devaluation, tariff protection and expansionary monetary and fiscal policy in order to boost domestic demand. Yet, these critics emphasise, it was the bankers' ideology – with its allegiance to the nineteenth-century liberal economy – that continued to dominate policy. The most notable illustration of this was the decision to return to the gold standard. This operated directly against the interests of industry. Such analysis has been attacked, in turn, as too simplistic. In particular, it has been suggested that the authorities were not narrowly sectarian but concerned for the broad interests of the country as a whole. Thus – it is said – the Bank of England sought to help industry and the unemployed through its advocacy of fixed exchange rates. Moreover, the banks' supporters point to the greater involvement with industry of a variety of financial institutions between the wars. This was true of the commercial banks, some merchant banks, and even the Bank of England, which was seen to undertake a pioneering role in the industrial rationalisation process. In addition, on the banks' side it must be stressed that despite major disruptions in international markets, Britain managed to avoid the devastating bank collapses of the sort that happened overseas. Moreover, despite persistently high unemployment rates, Britain's economic growth achievement during recovery from the Great Depression of 1929–32 was creditable in international terms. Critics of the banks are not satisfied, however. While they admit that there was greater involvement with industry during these years they, nevertheless, portray this as piecemeal and reluctant. For them, what was required was a wholesale redirection of British industrial investment. For the critics, the banks should have taken greater responsibility here, but between the wars they failed to do so.

It is clear from this very brief survey that there has been no reconciliation of the different views in the historical debate and, in fact, despite the major institutional, functional and technological changes that have occurred since World War II, there remains a similar controversy over the role of modern British financial institutions with respect to the needs of domestic industry. Inevitably, detailed criticism and rebuttal have altered somewhat from the debate on earlier periods but, in essence, the nature of the dissatisfaction is the same. Critically, for many decades from the 1950s Britain's long-term growth rate was poorer than that of other industrial nations (especially in Western Europe and Japan). So, too, was Britain's investment rate. Thus, discussion of a possible causal link has constantly re-emerged. For instance, the two major post-war enquiries into the operation of the financial system both investigated whether there were any serious market deficiencies in the provision of industrial funds (Radcliffe, 1960, *312, 322, 325–6*; Wilson, 1980, *32–3, 225, 263–8, 274–87*). One of the major post-war changes in the market has been the very sharp increase in the proportion of industrial company shares owned by financial institutions (in 1985, for instance, about 60 per cent of all UK company equities was held by insurance and pension funds and unit and investment trusts). Even so, there is still an oft-expressed suspicion that these institutions are more interested in short-term profits than in those long-term investments (for example, in research and development) needed to sustain high-technology industries. Parallel allegations are levied at the Stock Exchange – that investors are more concerned with making short-term gains than in encouraging companies to take the longer term view essential to maintaining Britain's international competitiveness. Broader criticisms also remain. Some critics continue to claim that banking ideology – with its loyalty to the open economy, to the maintenance of the City as an international centre, and to a strong currency and anti-inflationary policy – has continued to dominate British economic policy and that such dominance works against the long-term interests of British industry (Ingham, 1984; Pollard, 1982; Eatwell, 1982).

As for the earlier periods, economists who laud the operation of competitive markets are dismissive of allegations of failure. Yet the representative organ of industry, the Confederation of British Industry, has itself on occasions given expression to some doubts. Nevertheless, it is fair to say that its considered judgement has been to refute almost all the allegations made against the financial sector. In the mid-1980s, for instance, the CBI established a joint City/Industry Task Force which conducted a number of questionnaires and a series of conferences. Its unanimous conclusions were that the City was not seriously inhibiting industrial performance, financial institutions were not overly concerned with the short term, and that the banks *were* responsive to the needs of industrial companies (CBI, 1987). According to the Report, the cause of Britain's poor growth lay elsewhere, not least with industrialists themselves who, because of the general economic and political environment, have given insufficient weight to long-term developments irrespective of the influence of the City. The Task Force saw no easy solutions but rather lamely called for improved communications between the City and industry – a far cry from the radical 'solutions' preferred by many of the City's critics. In other words, both the modern and historical debates are still unresolved.

It is clear from the survey of the debate in this book that there can be no clear-cut, generally acceptable answer to the question: did the banks fail industry? The answer depends on many factors. The most basic of these is that often data do not exist in the form upon which to make a reliable judgement. Over and over again it has been surprising how commentators are prepared to make strong statements on the basis of little or inadequate evidence – a great deal of empirical work has yet to be done. More fundamentally, though, one's answer to the question depends upon the terms of reference being used. At its narrowest the debate has been concerned with testing and measuring the economic efficiency of financial markets. But, while such results on efficiency are important, they cannot in themselves be conclusive. It is clear that many commentators look far beyond the paradigm of market economics. In consequence, the apparently narrow discussion of the relationship between banks and industry has mushroomed into a vibrant, broad-ranging discussion which involves some of the fundamentals of British economic and social development. It is concerned with the composition of social elites, with the distribution of economic wealth and political power. Because of this, the debate continues to exercise the minds of economists, sociologists and political scientists but, above all, it provides fertile ground for the energies of the economic and social historian. The relationship between banks and industry is clearly an issue that can be but barely appreciated if bereft of the historical context.

Appendix

Recent contributions to the debate on the nature and extent of British bank involvement in the finance of industry can be grouped under three main heads: further exchanges on the role of the City; new research on the banks' archives; and a fuller picture of the European context within which British developments can be assessed.

On the wider socio-political role of bankers *vis à vis* industry (see Chapter 5), serious questions have been raised about the economic and political homogeneity of 'the City'. In particular, Daunton has argued that the interests of the individuals and the financial and commercial institutions that comprised 'the City' were diverse, sometimes in conflict and it is, thus, misleading to portray them as a clearly defined elite with common ethos and objectives (Daunton, 1989). He points, for instance, to evidence that contemporary responses to Chamberlain's proposals for tariff reform at the turn of the century found City bankers and importers in favour of free trade but City shipping and stock market interests favouring tariffs. He argues that the City did not speak with one voice and that it is a mistake to suggest it was the dominant, anti-industry force in British economic and social history that writers such as Ingham have argued. Rubinstein's estimates on the distribution of wealth amongst the very rich provide an important empirical underpinning for those who point to the continuing dominance of the City. Recent work has challenged the reliability of these estimates, however, and instead suggests that industrialists, after all, were not so weak relative to bankers and merchants (Daunton, *ibid.*; Berghoff, 1991; also see Nenadic, 1991). Differences of opinion persist, however. Rubinstein has re-asserted his claims about City wealth (see the exchange between Rubinstein and Daunton, 1991) and new research into financial elites in three European centres has re-stated the importance of a City aristocracy (Cassis, 1991). Moreover, a study of the reaction to the financial crisis of 1914 has offered some support for the view that the City did act in unison on important issues (Peters, 1993).

On the more specific question of the nature of bank involvement in the provision of finance for British industry, fresh archival research is beginning to offer more insight. Analysis of lending during the interwar years by two of Britain's biggest banks, the Midland and Lloyds, confirms that the commercial banks were drawn into deeper involvement with industrial customers during this troubled period (Ross, 1990). However, the evidence is such as to leave the banks open to the criticism that they could have done more to aid industrial rejuvenation, and new work on the Bank of England at that time also highlights the absence of a serious commitment to an industrial rationalisation programme (Bowden and Collins, 1992). This still leaves open the important question of whether or not it would have been beneficial to have had a greater commitment by the banks to an industrial rationalisation programme. Bank involvement in industrial decision-making is no guarantee of effective or efficient decisions. Preliminary results on bank lending to industry before 1914 confirm that commercial banks did lend routinely to industrial firms, that sometimes substantial amounts were involved and that nominally short term overdrafts were frequently renewed over numbers of years. In other words, it seems that the banks did more to support industry than some have given them credit for (Capie and Collins, 1991, 1992). However, this same research also confirms that British commercial banks did not own equity in their industrial customers' firms and that their entrepreneurial input into the running of those firms was minimal. In other words, their approach to industrial finance was arm's length, they were not universal banks of the type that existed in Germany towards the end of the nineteenth century.

Recent research on continental banking developments has, however, somewhat modified the comparative context in which British bank–industry relations are judged. A recent résumé of developments in Germany has endorsed the view that the banks in that country contributed in a significant manner to economic development before 1914 (Tilley, 1992). By the beginning of the twentieth century the large-scale German 'mixed' or 'universal' banks were providing venture capital for industry and were actively participating in the formation of new enterprises. However, it is a moot point whether German industry as a whole was better served by such banks. German banks at that time concentrated on providing finance and assistance to large companies, with a relative neglect of medium-sized and small firms (Tilley 1982; 1986). Moreover, German bank involvement with industry may have arisen from deficiencies in Germany's overall financial markets which were not present in the UK. From an early date, British industrialists had much larger and sophisticated financial markets to which to turn, even if they made little use of formal capital markets. A spate of new histories on banking developments in Europe has served to highlight the diversity of bank–industry relationships, but it, nonetheless, appears that some form of universal banking evolved in most northern and central European countries, with the major exceptions being France and Britain (James, Lindgren and Teichova, 1991; Teichova, Gourvish and Pogány, 1994). It is clear from these studies, however, that the banks took on an investment function largely because of inadequacies elsewhere in the provision of finance. In Britain, in contrast, the earlier maturation and larger size of financial markets conveyed important economies of scale and allowed greater specialisation of function among financial institutions. Moreover, British industrial firms remained largely self-financed, drawing little on outside sources of long-term funding (see pages 25–7). Even in Germany the closeness of the relationship between the big banks and big industry eased after the First World War, and the latest research on the post-Second World War period reveals a great deal of convergence in banking practice, with no sharp contrasts between Britain and Germany in the role that the banks have been playing in the finance of industry (Edwards and Fischer, 1994).

Finally, in assessing the relative merits of different banking systems, it is important to acknowledge the great stability exhibited by British credit banks. There were no major failures after 1878 and British stability during the interwar period was in stark contrast to experience on the Continent and in the USA, and this obviously conveyed important benefits to the rest of the British economy. This was partly due to the greater liquidity of British bank balance sheets, including their arm's length involvement with industrial clients. Indeed, one of the ironies that arises from an international comparison is that whereas in the interwar years British banks were being criticised for their failure to support fully British industry, banks on the Continent were being criticised for jeopardising the stability of the financial system through their deeper involvement with troubled sectors.

Notes

1. It is now widely accepted that the discontinuity exhibited in British growth rates during the late eighteenth and early nineteenth centuries was much less than seemed feasible to Gerschenkron and his contemporaries. A recent appraisal of the relevant figures appears in N. F. R. Crafts, *British Economic Growth during the Industrial Revolution* (Oxford, 1985), especially ch. 2.

2. The whole question of the magnitude and timing of any break in long-term growth rates at the turn of the century is itself still the subject of debate. A recent reappraisal of the debate can be found in Sidney Pollard, *Britain's Prime and Britain's Decline* (1989), ch. 1. A more technical treatment of the evidence is given in N. F. R. Crafts, S. J. Leybourne and T. C. Mills, 'The Climacteric in late Victorian Britain and France: a Reappraisal of the Evidence', *Journal of Applied Econometrics*, 4 (1989), *103–17*. However, even if it were conceded that there was no climacteric, the essence of the argument about banks and industry remains intact. The actual long-term growth rates achieved still generate disquiet and leave open the possibility that significant improvement might have been achieved if appropriate financial provision had been available.

3. An extremely useful starting point for those who may wish to look at the archives of nineteenth-century banks, including those of their own town and locality, is the study by L. S. Pressnell and John Orbell, *A Guide to the Historical Records of British Banking* (1985).

4. This estimate has itself been severely criticised: in particular, see Donald N. McCloskey's review of Kennedy's book, *Industrial Structure: Capital Markets and the Origins of British Economic Decline* (Cambridge, 1987) in *Economic History Review*, 42 (1989), *141–3*.

Bibliography

Aitken, J. (1970) 'Official Regulation of Overseas Investment, 1914–1931', *Economic History Review*, 23, 324–35.

Balogh, T. (1947) *Studies in Financial Organization* (Cambridge). Despite the date of publication, still a useful source of interwar financial markets.

Bamberg, James (1988) 'The Rationalisation of the British Cotton Industry in the Interwar Years', *Textile History*, 5. Details the restructuring problems facing this export industry; critical of the banks involvement.

Berghoff, Hartmut (1991) 'British Businessmen as Wealth-Holders 1870–1914: A Closer Look', *Business History*, 33, no. 2, 222–40.

Best, Michael H. and Jane Humphries (1986) 'The City and Industrial Decline' in Bernard Elbaum and William Lazonick (eds), *The Decline of the British Economy* (Oxford), pp. 223–39. Wide-ranging condemnation of the City's role *vis à vis* industry over the past century or more.

Bordo, Michael D. (1984) 'The Gold Standard: The Traditional Approach' in Michael D. Bordo and Anna J. Schwartz (eds), *A Retrospective on the Classical Gold Standard, 1821–1931*, pp. 23–229.

Bowden, Sue and Michael Collins (1992) 'The Bank of England, Industrial Regeneration, and Hire Purchase between the Wars', *Economic History Review*, 45, 120–36. Highlights the limited nature of the Bank of England's commitment to industrial intervention.

Cain, P. J. and A. G. Hopkins (1987) 'Gentlemanly Capitalism and British Expansion Overseas II: New Imperialism, 1850–1945', *Economic History Review*, 40, 1–26. Important survey, linking City attitudes to broader political and economic developments.

Cairncross, A. K. (1953) *Home and Foreign Investment, 1870–1913* (Cambridge).

Cameron, Rondo *et al.* (1967) *Banking in the Early Stages of Industrializa tion*. Concerned with the measurement of the growth of banking sectors during industrial development in a number of countries, including England and Scotland.

Capie, Forrest and Ghila Rodrik-Bali (1982) 'Concentration in British Banking, 1870–1920', *Business History*, 24, 280–92. Measuring the timing and scale of bank mergers.

Capie, Forrest (1988) 'Structure and Performance in British Banking, 1870–1939' in P. L. Cottrell and D. E. Moggridge (eds), *Money and Power*, pp. 73–102.

Capie, Forrest and Michael Collins (1991) 'Finance and Economic Activity in Britain, 1870–1914: preliminary observations', *Chiba Shodai Ronso*, 28, 159–77.

Capie, Forrest and Michael Collins (1992) *Have the Banks Failed British Industry?* A broad historical survey, 1870–1990.

Carrington, John C. and George T. Edwards (1979) *Financing Industrial Investment*. A study of the alleged weaknesses between finance and industry in contemporary Britain.

Cassis, Youssef (1985a) 'Management and Strategy in the English Joint-Stock Bank, 1890–1914', *Business History*, 27, 301–25. Emphasises the importance of private banks within the City.

Cassis, Youssef (1985b) 'Bankers in English Society in the Late Nine-teenth Century', *Economic History Review*, 38, 210–29. Highlights the importance of bankers (including those running the clearing banks) within the country's social and political elite.

Cassis, Y. (1991) 'Financial elites in three European centres: London, Paris, Berlin, 1880s–1930s', *Business History*, 33, no. 3, 53–71.

CBI (1987) *Investing for Britain's Future. Report of the City/Industry Task Force*. A brief report generally complimentary of the role of financial markets.

Chapman, Stanley P. (1970) 'Fixed Capital Formation in the British Cotton Industry, 1770–1815', *Economic History Review*, 23, 235–66.

Chapman, Stanley (1984) *The Rise of Merchant Banking*. The major general history of this important branch of the City in the years before World War I.

Checkland, S. G. (1975) *Scottish Banking. A History, 1695–1973* (Glasgow and London).

Church, Roy A. (1979) *Herbert Austin: The British Motor Car Industry to 1941*.

Clarke, William M. (1967). *The City in the World Economy*.

Clay, Henry (1929) *The Post-War Unemployment Problem*.

Collins, M. and Hudson, P. (1979) 'Provincial Bank Lending: Yorkshire and Merseyside, 1826–60', *Bulletin of Economic Research*, 31, 69–79. Uses bank archives to assess commercial industrial involvement of the banks in two important regions.

Collins, Michael (1984) 'The Business of Banking: English Bank Balance Sheets, 1840–80', *Business History*, 26, 43–58.

Collins, Michael (1988a) *Money and Banking in the UK. A History*. Wide ranging history of developments in banking and monetary policy.

Collins, Michael (1988b) 'English Banks and Business Cycles' in P. L. Cottrell and D. E. Moggridge (eds), *Money and Power*, pp. 1–39.

Collins, Michael (1989) 'The Banking Crisis of 1878', *Economic History Review*, 42, 504–27.

Cottrell, P. L. (1980) *Industrial Finance, 1830–1914. The Finance and Organization of English Manufacturing Industry*. An important appraisal of the sources of industrial finance before World War I.

Crick, W. F. and J. E. Wadsworth (1936) *A Hundred Years of Joint Stock Banking*.

Crouzet, François (1965) 'Capital Formation in Great Britain during the Industrial Revolution', *Second International Conference of Economic History (Aix-en-Provence)*, 2. A revised version is reprinted in Crouzet (1972).

Crouzet, François (ed.) (1972) *Capital Formation in the Industrial Revolution*. Extremely useful collection of essays on the topic.

Daunton, M. J. (1989) ' "Gentlemanly capitalism" and British industry, 1820–1914', *Past & Present*, 122, 119–58. Disputes the importance of the City in Britain's economy decline.

Daunton, M. J. (1991) ' "Gentlemanly capitalism" and British industry, 1820–1914: A Reply', *Past and Present*, 132, 170–87.

Dickson, P. G. M. (1960) *The Sun Insurance Office, 1710–1960*.

Dimsdale, D. H. (1981) 'British Monetary Policy and the Exchange Rate, 1920–1938' in W. A. Eltis and P. J. N. Sinclair (eds), 'The Money Supply and the Exchange Rate', Supplement to *Oxford Economic Papers*, 33, pp. 306–49. Succinct, balanced assessment of the course and impact of monetary policy between the wars.

Eatwell, John (1982) *Whatever Happened to Britain? The Economics of Decline*. A general onslaught against the debilitating influence of traditional attitudes and institutions – the banks and the City are amongst the targets.

Edelstein, Michael (1976) 'Realized Rates of Return on UK Home and Overseas Portfolio Investment in the Age of High Imperialism', *Explorations in Economic History*, 13, 283–329. This and the following reference constitute a carefully researched study which claims to exonerate the pre-1914 financial markets from any serious 'failures'.

Edelstein, Michael (1982) *Overseas Investment in the Age of High Imperialism. The United Kingdom, 1850–1914*.

Edwards, Jeremy and Fischer, Klaus (1994) *Banks, Finance and Investment in Germany* (Cambridge).

Elbaum, Bernard and William Lazonick (eds) (1986) *The Decline of the British Economy* (Oxford). An important collection of essays which collectively add credence to the editors' view that institutional constraints seriously damaged Britain's growth performance.

Ellinger, Barnard (1940) *The City. The London Financial Markets.*

Fetter, Frank Whitson (1965) *Development of British Monetary Orthodoxy, 1797–1875.* (Cambridge, Mass.). A careful study of the development of banking and monetary thought although it does not deal explicitly with the issue of the relationship between banks and industry.

Foreman-Peck, J. (1981) 'Exit, Voice and Loyalty as Responses to Decline: The Rover Company in the Inter-War Years', *Business History*, 23, 190–207.

Foster, John (1976) 'Imperialism and the Labour Aristocracy', in Jeffrey Skelley (ed.), *The General Strike*, pp. 3–57.

Foxwell, H. S. (1917) 'The Financing of Industry and Trade', *Economic Journal*, 27, 502–22. An early, well-publicised condemnation of the banks' neglect of industry.

Gerschenkron, Alexander (1966) *Economic Backwardness in Historical Perspective. A Book of Essays* (Cambridge, Mass.), 2nd impression. At the time of publication, a major contribution to the analysis of the industrial development process in Europe.

Gilbart, J. W. (1911) *The History, Principles and Practice of Banking*, 2 vols, ed. Ernest Sykes.

Goodhart, C. A. E. (1972) *The Business of Banking, 1891–1914.* An empirical investigation of the London clearing banks' balance sheets.

Green, Edwin and Michael Moss (1982) *A Business of National Importance. The Royal Mail Shipping Group, 1892–1937.* Provides useful case study of the rationalisation process facing important sections of industry between the wars.

Griffiths, Brian (1973) 'The Development of Restrictive Practices in the UK Monetary System', *Manchester School*, 41, 3–18.

Hannah, Leslie (1976) *The Rise of the Corporate Economy.*

Harris, Jose and Pat Thane (1984) 'British and European Bankers, 1880–1914: an "Aristocratic" Bourgeoisie', in Pat Thane *et al.*, *The Power of the Past. Essays for Eric Hobsbaum* (Cambridge).

Harrison, A. E. (1982) 'F. Hopper and Co. The Problems of Capital Supply in the Cycle Manufacturing Industry, 1891–1914', *Business History*, 24, 3–23. One of the few journal articles that explicitly addresses the issue of the adequacy of capital supply in a 'new industry' of the late nineteenth century.

Hilferding, Rudolf (1910, trans. 1981) *Finance Capital. A Study of the Latest Phase of Capitalist Development*, edited by Tom Bottomore from translations by Morris Watnick and Sam Gordon. A difficult but important starting point in the long Marxist bibliography.

Holmes, A. R. and Edwin Green (1986) *Midland. 150 years of Banking History.* An important 'in-house' history of one of the leading clearing banks.

Howson, Susan (1988) 'Cheap Money and Debt Management in Britain, 1932–51', in P. L. Cottrell and D. E. Moggridge (eds), *Money and Power*, pp. 227–89.

Hudson, Pat (1981) 'The Role of Banks in the Finance of the West Yorkshire Wool Textile Industry, c. 1780–1850', *Business History Review*, 55, 379–402.

Hudson, Pat (1986) *The Genesis of Industrial Capital. A Study of the West Riding Wool Textile Industry c. 1750–1850* (Cambridge). This and the previous reference use archive material to study the problem of capital supply in one of the country's leading industries.

Hume, John R. and Michael S. Moss (1979) *Beardmore. The History of a Scottish Industrial Giant.*

Hume, L. J. (1963) 'The Gold Standard and Deflation: Issues and Attitudes in the Nineteen-Twenties', *Economica*, 30, 225–42; reproduced in Pollard (1970), pp. 122–45.

Ingham, Geoffrey (1984) *Capitalism Divided? The City and Industry in British Social Development.* Stresses the commercial function of the City and how this has hindered the industrial interests of the country.

Johnson, H. G. (1951) 'Some Implications of Secular Changes in Bank Assets and Liabilities in Great Britain', *Economic Journal 61*, 544–61.

Kennedy, William P. (1974) 'Foreign Investment, Trade and Growth in the United Kingdom, 1870–1913', *Explorations in Economic History*, 11, 415–44.

Kennedy, William P. (1976) 'Institutional Response to Economic Growth: Capital Markets in Britain to 1914', in Leslie Hannah (ed.), *Management Strategy and Business Development. An Historical and Comparative Study*, pp. 151–83.

Kennedy, William P. (1987) *Industrial Structure, Capital Markets and the Origins of British Economic Decline* (Cambridge). This and the previous two references represent one of the most important arguments that pre-1914 financial markets 'failed', and at a high cost to industrial and general economic growth.

Keynes, J. M. (1931) 'The Economic Consequences of Mr. Churchill', reproduced in Pollard (1970), pp. 27–43.

Killick, J. R. and W. A. Thomas (1970) 'The Provincial Stock Exchanges, 1830–1870', *Economic History Review*, 23, 96–111.

Kirby, Maurice W. (1974) 'The Lancashire Cotton Industry in the

Interwar Years. A Study in Organisation Change', *Business History*, 16, 145–59.

Leaf, Walter (1926) *Banking*.

Lenin, V. I. (1969 reprint) 'Imperialism: The Highest Stage of Capitalism' in Progress Publishers (eds), *Selected Works*, pp. 176–263.

Longstreth, Frank (1979) 'The City, Industry and the State' in Colin Crouch (ed.), *State and Economy in Contemporary Capitalism*, pp. 157–90.

Macmillan (1931) Committee on Finance and Industry. *Report*, cmd. 3897; and *Minutes of Evidence*, 2 vols. The most important official enquiry into the topic between the wars.

Mathias, Peter (1973) 'Capital, Credit and Enterprise in the Industrial Revolution', *Journal of European Economic History*, 2, 121–43.

Matthews, K. G. P. (1986) 'Was Sterling Overvalued in 1925?', *Economic History Review*, 39, 572–87.

Michie, R. C. (1981) 'Options, Concessions, Syndicates, and the Provision of Venture Capital, 1880–1913', *Business History*, 23, 147–64. Careful presentation of the view that the influence of financial markets was benign.

Michie, R. C. (1987) *The London and New York Stock Exchanges, 1850–1914*. Essential reading for a survey of developments in the formal market for capital.

Moggridge, D. E. (1972) *British Monetary Policy, 1924–1931* (Cambridge).

Morgan, E. V. and Thomas, W. A. (1962) *The Stock Exchange: Its History and Functions*.

Munn, Charles W. (1981) *The Scottish Provincial Banking Companies 1747–1864* (Edinburgh).

Nenadic, Stana (1991) 'Businessmen, the Urban Middle Class, and the "Dominance" of Manufacturers in Nineteenth-Century Britain', *Economic History Review*, 44, 66–85.

Nevin, Edward (1955) *The Mechanism of Cheap Money* (Cardiff).

Ollerenshaw, Philip (1987) *Banking in Nineteenth-Century Ireland. Belfast Banks, 1825–1914* (Manchester).

Overbeek, Hans (1980) 'Finance Capital and the Crisis in Britain', *Capital and Class*, 11, 99–120. Attempts to show that the convergence of financial and industrial interests was long delayed in UK – until 1970s.

Payne, Peter L. (1979) *Colvilles and the Scottish Steel Industry* (Oxford).

Perkins, Edwin J. C. (1975) *Financing Anglo-American Trade. The House of Brown, 1800–1880* (Cambridge, Mass.). The history of one of the leading merchant banks of last century.

Peters, John (1993) 'The British Government and the City–Industry Divide', *Twentieth-Century British History*, 4, 126–48.

Pollard, Sidney (1964) 'Fixed Capital in the Industrial Revolution in

Britain', *Journal of Economic History*, 24, 299–314. Reprinted in Crouzet (1972). A pioneering article on the topic.

Pollard, Sidney (1970) 'Introduction' in Sidney Pollard (ed.), *The Gold Standard and Employment Policies between the Wars*, pp. 1–26.

Pollard, Sidney (1982) *The Wasting of the British Economy*. Lively polemic which lists the City as one of the culprits in Britain's poor post-war growth record.

Pollard, Sidney (1985) 'Capital Exports: Harmful or Beneficial?', *Economic History Review*, 38, 489–514. A wide-ranging survey of the literature on the effects of Britain's pre-1914 overseas investment.

Pollard, Sidney (1989) *Britain's Prime and Britain's Decline. The British Economy, 1870–1914*. A broad 'pessimistic' appraisal of the performance of the late Victorian and Edwardian economy.

Presnell, L. S. (1956) *Country Banking in the Industrial Revolution* (Oxford). Still the authority for this early period.

Radcliffe (1960) Committee on the Working of the Monetary System. *Report*, Cmnd. 827. A major enquiry into the country's financial markets and institutions but largely from the perspective of the operation of policy rather than the financing of industry.

Rae, George (1988) *The Country Banker* (7th edn).

Redmond, John (1984) 'The Sterling Overvaluation in 1925. A Multilateral Approach', *Economic History Review*, 37, 520–32.

Rubinstein, W. D. (1976) 'The Victorian Middle Classes: Wealth, Occupation, and Geography', *Economic History Review*, 30, 602–23. This and the following references comprise a major study which – amongst other things – highlights the wealth of the banking and commercial classes during the nineteenth century.

Rubinstein, W. D. (1977) 'Wealth, Elites and the Class Structure of Modern Britain', *Past & Present*, 76, 99–126.

Rubinstein, W. D. (1986) *Wealth and Inequality in Britain*.

Rubinstein, W. D. (1991) '"Gentlemanly Capitalism" and British Industry, 1820–1914', *Past & Present*, 132, 150–70.

Saville, J. (1961) 'Some Retarding Factors in the British Economy before 1914', *Yorkshire Bulletin of Economic and Social Research*, 13, 51–9. A 'pessimistic' view of British industrial performance.

Sayers, R. S. (1938) *Modern Banking* (Oxford). For many years a standard text.

Sayers, R. S. (1957) *Central Banking after Bagehot* (Oxford).

Sayers, R. S. (1960) 'The Return to Gold', in L. S. Pressnell (ed.), *Studies in the Industrial Revolution*; reproduced in Pollard (1970), pp. 85–98.

Sayers, R. S. (1976) *The Bank of England, 1891–1944* (Cambridge), 3 vols. The official history of the Bank. The chapters on the interwar period are particularly useful on the Bank's involvement in attempts at industrial rationalisation.

Scammell, W. M. (1968) *The London Discount Market* (New York).

Sheppard, David K. (1971) *The Growth and Role of UK Financial Institutions, 1880–1962.*

Supple, Barry (1970) *The Royal Exchange Assurance. A History of British Insurance, 1720–1970* (Cambridge).

Supple, Barry (ed.) (1977) *Essays in British Business History.* (Oxford).

Taylor, Arthur J. (1972) *Laissez-faire and State Intervention in Nineteenth-Century Britain.*

Thomas, S. Evelyn (1931) *British Banks and the Finance of Industry.*

Thomas, W. A. (1973) *The Provincial Stock Exchanges.* The authoritative history of these exchanges.

Thomas, W. A. (1978) *The Finance of British Industry, 1918–1976.* Provides essential institutional framework and details of changes in market practice.

Tilley, R. H. (1986) 'German Banking, 1850–1914: Development Assistance for the Strong', *Journal of European Economic History*, 15, 113–51.

Tolliday, Steven (1987) *Business, Banking and Politics. The Case of British Steel. 1918–1936.* A major industrial study concentrating on the problems of restructuring in these troubled years; highlighting and criticising the role of the banks and of the state.

Truptil, R. J. (1936) *British Banks and the London Money Market.*

Wilson (1980) Committee to Review the Functioning of Financial Institutions. *Report and Appendices*, Cmnd. 7937. The most recent wide-ranging enquiry into financial markets and institutions. There is explicit discussion of the industry/bank relationship.

Winton, J. R. (1982) *Lloyds Bank, 1918–1969* (Oxford). An 'official' history of one of the leading clearing banks.

Index

New Studies in Economic and Social History

Titles in the series available from Cambridge University Press:

Previously published as

Studies in Economic History

Titles in the series available from the Macmillan Press Limited

Economic History Society

The Economic History Society, which numbers around 3,000 members, publishes the *Economic History Review* four times a year (free to members) and holds an annual conference.

Enquiries about membership should be addressed to

The Assistant Secretary
Economic History Society
PO Box 70
Kingswood
Bristol
BS15 5TB

Full-time students may join at special rates.